50 Sports Strategies to Out-Think, Out-Train, and
Out-Perform Your Competition

★

TRAIN TOUGH THE ARMY WAY

MARK BENDER

Lieutenant Colonel (Ret.)
United States Army

Contemporary Books

Chicago   New York   San Francisco   Lisbon   London   Madrid   Mexico City
Milan   New Delhi   San Juan   Seoul   Singapore   Sydney   Toronto

Library of Congress Cataloging-in-Publication Data

Bender, Mark C. (Mark Christian), 1951–
     Train tough the army way : 50 sports strategies to out-think, out-train, and out-perform your competition / Mark Bender.
        p.   cm.
     ISBN 0-07-140808-8
     1. Athletes—Training of.   2. Athletes—Psychology.   3. United States.
Army—Physical training.   I. Title.

GV711.5 .B46   2002

2002074001

2 3 4 5 6 7 8 9 0   AGM/AGM   1 0 9 8 7 6 5 4 3 2

ISBN 0-07-140808-8

Interior design by Nick Panos
Cover photograph copyright © ABStudio/Workbookstock.com

McGraw-Hill books are available at special quantity discounts to use as premiums and sales promotions, or for use in corporate training programs. For more information, please write to the Director of Special Sales, Professional Publishing, McGraw-Hill, Two Penn Plaza, New York, NY 10121-2298. Or contact your local bookstore.

This book is printed on acid-free paper.

Dedicated to Sam Bender

Stellar second baseman. Hunter of U-boats in the North Atlantic. Pro sports chapel visionary. Athlete, coach, and counselor. Preacher, teacher, and personality. Mentor to the stars. Friend to the little guy.

Who took me to the games and showed me what to look for. Who sent me forth to camps and clinics in search of the edge. Who understood that for people like us, sports are who we are, an essential part of our manhood, and an important venue for character-building.

And he made it all fun.

Thanks, Dad.

CONTENTS

PART FOUR Face the New World

PART FIVE Ultimate Weapons

FOREWORD

I knew Mark Bender when he was a skinny little kid—kind of a runt, really.

I played Triple A for the Toledo Mud Hens for a season and met his father, Sam Bender, early in my career. Sam was a close friend of Bobby Richardson, then an All-Star second baseman with the Yankees. Toledo was the Yankees' farm club at the time, as well as the hometown of the Bender clan. So it was a natural relationship, and the Benders took me under wing.

Sam had been around the Yankees a lot up to that point, a place I was hoping to go. He told me right away that I would fit in, that he thought I had what it took to play major league ball—even with the New York Yankees. That meant a lot, having someone believe in me.

Mark was another story. I was five or six years older than Mark was, and I think he kind of looked at me as a surrogate older brother. He came at me pretty hard. As I say, he was a skinny kid, about 12 at the time, but he had attitude. Mark was an edge man. We played Ping-Pong, one-on-one basketball, golf, and a bunch of games of his own invention. He usually invented the rules, too. It was obvious he was a very competitive athlete and very in tune with the mental side of sports. He already had a room full of trophies and ribbons he had won at various sports camps. Oh yeah, his room had a broken window, too, the result of his having batted a rubber ball through it.

Mark and his dad would come to games periodically, and we'd always visit a bit. I'd often see them in Detroit, Cleveland, or Chicago. But one time Mark called me while the team was in Kansas City. We had breakfast together in the old Muehlebach Hotel, where the Yankees stayed at the time. The year was 1973, and Mark had one of those long, almost hippie hairstyles that were in vogue at the time. He offered to drive me to the ballpark for batting practice.

He picked me up an hour later, minus the hair.

Turns out Mark was on his way to officer boot camp at Fort Riley, Kansas. I was shocked. Having spent a couple Vietnam-era years in the Army myself, it was not a career I was recommending at the time. After all, I had been drafted. But it was something he wanted to do, and I figured he would do it well.

I should have known he'd find a way to juggle his military duties with an active sports life.

What the world gets out of this unique synthesis is the revolutionary sports strategy in *Train Tough the Army Way*. Mark has studied at the premier military institutions. He's taught at the finest military schools. And he's taken what he's learned and applied it all to the world of the athlete. The strategies are totally unique in this regard.

After stints with the San Francisco Giants and the Chicago Cubs, I returned to finish out my career with the New York Yankees. I hadn't seen Mark in several years, although I heard good things about his Army service. He'd been assigned to Holland for duty, not surprisingly, as a sports officer. There he'd been named Officer of the Year for Headquarters, Allied Forces Central Europe.

When he returned from Holland, Mark was the featured speaker at a Yankees team gathering in Cleveland. I could see where the soldier approach to sports performance was already taking shape. Mark is a dynamic speaker, and a lot of what he said that day hit home with the team. With Mark Bender you get the essential information without a lot of the extraneous stuff. He gets to the point and moves on.

Pay attention. What he has to say could change your life.

Bobby Murcer

ACKNOWLEDGMENTS

I would like to thank my family for their support throughout this endeavor: Heidi for her love and patience; Jim for his eager review of each chapter; Bob for the section on hyperization; Lisa for her soccer courage; and Matt for his help with the title and concept. Good job, people; take the rest of the day off. We move out again in the morning.

It was a pleasure to work with Betsy Lancefield Lane, senior editor at Contemporary Books, whose creative thinking greatly influenced the Train Tough strategy. I owe her a lot. Managing editor Marisa L'Heureux was helpful at every turn and a real pro. Project editor Katherine Dennis kept everything running ahead of schedule.

This project would not have been possible without the assistance of a number of consummate professionals, among them my brother, Tom Bender, who carefully reviewed each chapter; Donna Martin, whose instruction and mentorship on the publishing business proved invaluable; American Biography general counsel Nick Winter, for his guidance and legal advice; Steve Brown at the U.S. Army Combined Arms Research Library, for his manuscript review; and psychiatrist Dr. Mary Beth Arms, who gave the manuscript a thorough sanity check while giving the author a free pass.

Special thanks to Marlys Arnold, Rick Atkinson, Ernie Barrett, Marilyn Bender, Bill Brooks, Marlin and Linda Cone, Jud Donahue, Gary Eckert, Jerry Fogel at KPHN, Bill Hart, Joanne Honeycutt, David Hopkins, Kelly Jones, Patricia King, Norma Lamp, Warren and Anneliese Lott, Tim Nenninger, Shirley Rickett, Clarence Roberts, Dan Roberts at KMBZ, Vickie Spencer, Myra Sturm, Karla Thrush, Jon and Ruth Ann Wefald, and Mike Word at the *Kansas City Star*.

I want to recognize the heroes in my life: mentors Sheldon Bassett, Thom Brownworth, Hallie Bryant, Monte Clarke, Marion Crawley, Van Crouch, Harve Chrouser, Bob Davenport, Donn Gaebelein, Bill Glass, Marvin Goldberg, Jim Gordon, Steve Hamilton, Bill Hart, Jerry Kendall, Tony Kubek, Mickey Mantle, Bobby Murcer, Don Odle, Lee Pfund, Bobby Richardson, Charlie Scales, Johnny Spence, Watson Spoelstra, Frank Stranahan, Ned Stuckey, Dave Swanson, Paul Wiggin, Bud Williams, Dick Wilson, Tex Winter, Al Worthington, and Billy Zeoli. Almost every one of these great men I came to know through my father, hero, and mentor Sam Bender.

I pay tribute to the many great thinkers who influenced the Train Tough strategy, including Robert Allen, Tod Barnhart, Charles Belitz, Yogi Berra, Brian Biro, Ken Blanchard, Laurence Boldt, Les Brown, Carlos Castaneda, Stephen Covey, Danny Cox, Robert Grudin, Lou Holtz, Phil Jackson, Bob Lemon, Vince Lombardi, Richard Marcinko, Rollo May, Bill Parcells, Rick Pitino, Pat Riley, Anthony Robbins, Jim Rohm, Peter Senge, Don Shula, Carl Vuono, John Wooden, and Zig Ziglar.

The following provided background for many of the vignettes through which I lived: *The World Series* by Donald Honig, *Neil Leifer's Sports Stars* by Peter Bonventre, *Basketball* by Jim Benagh, *When All the World Was Browns Town* by Terry Pluto, and *The Mick* by Mickey Mantle with Herb Gluck. Joe Posnanski at the *Kansas City Star* and Jack McCallum at *Sports Illustrated* did a great job exploring the Rulon Gardner phenomenon. Peter King's *Sports Illustrated* article "Bitter Pill," was helpful in documenting Brett Favre's successful struggle with painkillers.

Defeat into Victory by Field Marshal Viscount William Slim was critical to understanding one of the great campaigns of World War II, and *Churchill: A Life* by Martin Gilbert provided useful insights into the life and career of Sir Winston. *The End of Marketing as We Know It* by Sergio Zyman is an incredible book in its own right, and it influenced both my marketing approach to *Train Tough* as well as the attitude I brought to the work itself. *Psycho-Cybernetics* by Maxwell Maltz was the bible I used on visualization.

A number of highly professional works kept me on track where the issues were complex: *The Quiet Storm* by Alexandra Powe-Allred and Michelle Powe; *Raising Our Athletic Daughters* by Jean Zimmerman and Gil Reavill; *Sports and Athletes: Opposing Viewpoints* edited by Laura Egendorf (Mariah Nelson's essay was especially enlightening); *Why Johnny Hates Sports* by Fred Engh; *Body for Life* by Bill Phillips and Michael D'Orso; *Fit Happens* by Joannie Greggains with Patricia Romanowski; *Uppers, Downers, All Arounders* by Daryl Inaba, William Cohen, and Michael Holstein; and *The Betty Ford Center Book of Answers* by James West.

The following organizations also deserve thanks: the Negro Leagues Museum, City of Lake Lotawana, The Writer's Place, University of Missouri at Kansas City, Park Hill High School, Kansas City Public Library, Mid-Continent Public Library, U.S. Army Combined Arms Research Library, Weatherby Lake Writer's Guild, Maple Woods Community College, Southern Platte County Athletic Association, Pine Ridge Presbyterian Church, U.S. Army War College, and the U.S. Army Combined Arms Center and Fort Leavenworth.

Finally, thanks to fellow warriors Al Davis, Jack Lamey, Norman Robbins, Scott Wedman, "the Ridge" softball team, and all the guys at Harney Gym—past and present.

INTRODUCTION

★

Three bears and a crocodile. Every man reacted differently. Some fought gamely to the bitter end. Some called on the gods for deliverance. Some surrendered and were devoured. Only a few were prepared for the moment. Only a few mastered their weaponry, conquered their fear, and harnessed their will to survive.

For seven hundred years the Roman Empire sponsored gladiatorial contests. It was a vicious, bloodthirsty time. Gladiators played for keeps. Failure often meant death.

But there were ways out of this grisly system. Some gladiators escaped, some rebelled, and some perfected their craft to the point where they were rewarded with their freedom. Successful gladiators had a plan, a picture in their mind of where they wanted to go, and a detailed strategy for getting there.

If you were one of the 85 million or so who packed theaters to see *Gladiator*, you recall the main character, Maximus, was a military man, accomplished in the art of war. It was only when the politics went bad that he was thrust into the arena as a gladiator. There his leadership and battle skills soon became apparent, and he was able to harness what he knew from the battlefield and use it in the arena.

Like Maximus, many gladiators were captured soldiers, who learned their skills in the military. They brought with them the tactics and strategies that achieved success on the battlefield.

There's always been a powerful connection between military strategy and sports. But up until now the two have largely existed in parallel universes—which is ridiculous. Sports are a simulation of the battleground, a healthy way to vent, and a great way to burn off our aggressive tendencies in a controlled environment. Football is the classic example with its "aerial attacks," "blitzes," and "the bomb." But all sports are a battle.

The way soldiers prepare for conflict is very similar to the way athletes prepare for a game. Because the stakes are higher and the environment more chaotic in actual combat, a lot of thought has gone into military strategy down through the ages. And a lot of that thought applies to athletes and the teams we play on.

There are too many high-potential athletes wandering around out there letting situations dictate to them . . .

I won't glamorize war or the taking of human life. But we're fools if we don't take full advantage of the lessons of U.S. military offers and the tactics, training, and leadership strategies that lead to success. It's like what NASA points out about space exploration: it's not just what you learn about space, it's also the things you learn in getting there—things that can be used in other ways.

As athletes, we need to find a new way of thinking about sports performance. We need to think more clearly about what we're doing and get motivated about reaching the next level. There are too many high-potential athletes wandering around out there letting situations dictate to them, rather than demonstrating a coherent strategy that

1 TRAIN TOUGH

The Train Tough strategy is a powerful way of thinking—based on the way soldiers going into combat need to think. The strategy controls everything. The strategy will take you from "see what happens" to "make it happen." It uses every factor affecting outcome and turns it to your advantage. It's always looking for that edge . . . regardless of what sport you play.

has an impact on their game. We need to quit fooling around and get our minds right.

It doesn't matter if you're in synchronized swimming or Golden Glove boxing. Whether your sport is a team sport like lacrosse or an individual sport like distance running. All sports are impacted by strategy.

I want to blast open a new way of thinking and light your fire. I want to give you sports strategies that will change your life. As athletes we know we're facing ever-increasing competition, but no one is offering a coherent strategy on how to think about this challenge. I'm going to be chucking hand grenades and laying down machine-gun fire to get you moving. And you don't have to join the Army to reap the benefit.

I've already done that for you.

As a lieutenant colonel in the United States Army, I devoted my professional life to getting ready for the next war, mastering the art and science of the battlefield, and training soldiers for the stress of combat. I taught at some of the Army's premier leadership schools and commanded a unit that prepped soldiers for Desert Storm. What I found was that many of the qualities that make a good soldier are also found in winning athletes. There are key similarities between the battlefield and the playing field.

There are key similarities between the battlefield and the playing field.

Though I became a professional soldier, I was groomed to be an athlete.

From the age of three, my dad pitched softballs to me in the backyard. The porch screen was the backstop. Every time I missed, the ball hit the porch screen and Mom would yell out to knock it off. It was hit the ball or else.

I grew up as a runt, smaller than the other kids.

I was gifted with quickness, good reactions, and an unrelenting drive to win. At sports camps I always brought home the ribbons—Ping-Pong, box hockey, tennis, miniature golf, home-run derby, you name it. If there was a competition, I was out there figuring the angles. Runts make good students; we have to learn quickly just to survive.

As a kid I was privileged to have an inside track on two of the great professional teams of the '60s—the New York Yankees and Cleveland Browns. My dad was close to players on both teams. I watched All-Pro defensive end Bill Glass using the then-revolutionary psycho-cybernetics to get "up" for a game; I watched Mickey Mantle knock down Miller High Lifes in the Yankees locker room after a game—a telltale sign of problems to come.

My father taught me the power of observation. We never went to a game without his Navy binoculars. We learned to tell who was going to hit and who was just taking his cuts. Who was going to knock down a free throw and who was going to choke. Who had big-league potential and who didn't.

When I finally hit puberty, Dad took me to workouts with Frank Stranahan, a tremendous bodybuilder and golfer. Frank was way ahead of his time, using weight training and a running program to enhance his health and athletic career. Frank must have seen something in me early on; he hired me as a sports trainer for his son, Jimmy. So at age 16 I was building a new body and reviewing sports fundamentals in the best possible way—as a personal trainer.

Throughout my career, I've played two, three, and sometimes four team sports a year, often as a player-coach. Basketball, baseball, football, and volleyball have been my main events, with plenty of golf and tennis mixed in. I've trained for sprints and distance-running competitions and competed in badminton, table tennis, and handball

2 SELECT A TARGET

As an athlete, target selection is part of your job. It's your job to define your destination and develop a strategy for getting there. Your destination is where you want to be, not a mythical maybe-land of see-what-happens. Once you know the target, you can focus your efforts on hitting it—and blasting through to the other side.

events. I've coached and played soccer and had training in swimming and gymnastics. My sons are wrestlers, so I've had a pretty good look inside this most demanding of sports. I lived in Holland for three years where I played European handball with the natives. I could go on. Sports are my life; finding a way to win is my quest.

I've always wanted to know the strategies for success.

When I learned that President Dwight Eisenhower called his year at the Army's Leavenworth School "a watershed in my life," I wanted to find out why. How did a young major, told by his superiors that he "would probably fail," wind up the number one graduate in his class? How did he do it? What were his strategies?

When I found out, I wrote a book about it. And guess what? The strategies that propelled the life of Eisenhower are the same strategies that will propel your success as an athlete.

I wrote another book called *Trial by Basketball: The Life and Times of Tex Winter*. Exploring Coach Winter's life was an awesome experience. Here's a man who coached Michael Jordan longer than any other coach, who is Phil Jackson's basketball guru, and who in his eighties is a vital assistant

> *Sports are my life; finding a way to win is my quest.*

with the world champion Los Angeles Lakers. Coach Tex Winter is a man with a strategy, and he taught me a lot.

The strategies presented in this book are gleaned from a lifetime of seasons and competitions. I'll show you the trophies . . . and the scars. The Train Tough strategy was conceived in the mind, channeled through the heart, and tested on the playing field.

The Train Tough Strategy

The Train Tough strategy is a powerful way of thinking—based on the way soldiers going into combat need to think. The strategy controls everything. It will take you from "see what happens" to "make it happen." The Train Tough strategy uses every factor affecting outcome and turns it to your advantage. It's always looking for that edge . . . regardless of what sport you play.

As an athlete, target selection is part of your job. It's your job to define your destination and develop a strategy for getting there. Your destination is where you want to be, not a mythical maybe-land of see-what-happens. Once you know the target, you can focus your efforts on hitting it—and blasting through to the other side.

Train Tough is a unique, high-speed, and effective sports strategy.

I'm going to challenge you right from Jump Street. We're going to find out how bad you want it. We're going to get your mind right and teach you how to walk like a winner, think like a warrior, and perform like a hero. You'll make the team, practice for perfection, and learn how to lead. You'll know your enemy like the back of your hand. You'll be ready, *really* ready. You'll learn every nuance of game time—and how to achieve top performance when it counts.

You'll learn how to prepare for competition, optimize performance, and peak at crunch time. Whether in individual or team sports, the strategies will give you a decisive edge. This is not a book for eggheads; there are no charts or graphs—just the hard-boiled facts of life in the arena, from a guy who's been there.

We'll tackle the tough issues—sex, drugs, and the party train. You'll learn from the great ones and check out what's happening in women's sports. Finally, we'll motivate you for the hyper state and get you stoked to set up shop in the amazing business of sports.

Train Tough the Army Way will motivate you to achieve supremacy in any and every sport you play. It will reinforce what you've already experienced and give you a whole new outlook on the game. You'll get instruction on visualization techniques, gamesmanship, and conditioning. Along the way you'll experience a variety of sporting events, military campaigns, and the perspectives of great athletes—and see how those lessons apply in the arenas of today.

There's also a moral aspect to the Train Tough strategy. Your morals. When the conscience buzzer goes off, you have to make the call. The boundaries are there; you have to negotiate the gray areas. The strategy can't provide character, but it does recognize the need for it. We all have to live with ourselves and the society we create by our actions. We play hard. We have the attitude of the warrior. But we keep it on the high road.

---

3 TAKE THE HIGH ROAD

There's a moral aspect to the Train Tough strategy. Your morals. When the conscience buzzer goes off, you have to make the call. The boundaries are there; you have to negotiate the gray areas. The strategy can't provide character, but it does recognize the need for it. We all have to live with ourselves and the society we create by our actions. We play hard. We have the attitude of the warrior. But we keep it on the high road.

The Train Tough strategy also applies to life. Sports performance is a lot like life performance. Walking into a gym is not that different from walking into a classroom or a new job. The question isn't, "What's going to happen?" It's "What do I have to do to get an A?" Or, "How many sales until I get the Lexus?"

As you master Train Tough strategies on the sports field, the applications to your life situation will become obvious. The good habits you develop will strengthen your performance; bad habits will add friction that make achievement difficult. Every habit builds on every other habit. Good training habits make for good study and career habits. Good sportsmanship habits make for good citizenship habits. Habits build on each other. Identify, break down, and destroy bad habits; identify, build, and reinforce good habits.

There are shortcuts to every Train Tough strategy. But don't waste time looking for them. Stay on the path, building strength along the journey, always looking for a better way.

Decide now what you want your future to be, so we can begin sharpening the weapons you'll need to get there.

How to Use This Book

I'm a guy who believes the history of the universe is reducible to the back of a 3″ × 5″ card. I like to keep things simple. To my mind, if most of the learning situations in life lasted half as long, they would be twice as effective. *Train Tough* is short and sweet for exactly that reason. You're getting the essential Train Tough strategies; think of it this way—you'll actually have time to train.

Train Tough the Army Way is more concerned with *how* you think than *what* you think. If how you think is improved, you can define the details of what you think on your own. For instance, I have my view of sports nutrition, and sports nutrition is important and something you need to think about because it will affect how you perform. Yet my section on the subject will be relatively simple. You'll get the basics, and you'll be motivated to find out more on your own. There are many good books on the subject; this will not be one of them.

I'm on a different mission: shaping how you think. If we can affect your thinking process, the rest is relatively simple. You'll be able to take the strategies and apply them to every sport you play, in every situation you find yourself.

Go ahead and write in this book—unless it's a library book. In that case, go buy a personal copy. It'll be worth it. Underline the salient points. Reread key passages before a workout, practice, or competition. I found that my sports performance peaked while putting *Train Tough* together. It got me juiced. Soak it in—again and again.

Use this book like a mirror—to view where you are today in your sports life and to formulate how you're going to get where you want to be tomorrow.

4 MAKE IT A HABIT

Good habits strengthen performance; bad habits add friction that makes achievement difficult. Every habit builds on every other habit. Good training habits make for good study and career habits. Good sportsmanship habits make for good citizenship habits. Habits build on each other. Identify, break down, and destroy bad habits; identify, build, and reinforce good habits.

At the end of each chapter is a Train Tough Challenge. Take these challenges. I won't ask you to do something I wouldn't do or haven't already done. Get used to meeting challenges. You're going to face a lot of them before you're through. Meet the Train Tough Challenges as we move along, and by the end, you'll be ready to take on the world.

I promise you, *Train Tough* will not be boring.

Because I bore easily, I have an almost paranoiac fear of boring others. I write in the Army style—short, to the point, bottom line up front—no bull. It's "Dudley simple," so Dudley over there understands it. Let's get on with it.

TRAIN TOUGH CHALLENGE

Read on.

PART ONE

GET YOUR MIND RIGHT
DECIDE WHAT YOU WANT
AND HOW BAD YOU WANT IT

1

HOW BAD DO YOU WANT IT?

★

Most people try things. I don't. As Yoda taught Luke Skywalker, there is no try. There is either do or do not.

—ROBERT G. ALLEN

How bad do you want it?

How bad do you want to achieve excellence in the sports you play? Are you gunning for the top or just putting in time? Do you have goals? Or are you waiting to see what happens?

Go ahead, be honest. How bad do you want it? What kind of effort are you willing to put in? Fifty percent? Seventy-five percent? Ninety percent?

A "maybe I'll go out for football" puts you at 50 percent. You might be a pretty good athlete, but you're not sure about the hard work, the hits you'll have to take, and the risk of injury. You're probably not doing a lot of preseason conditioning. Training camp is going to be a real bear. Maybe Grandma bought you *Train Tough* hoping to light a fire under your fanny. You may or may not finish this book—there are a lot of distractions out there, like TV and video games.

A good player is at 75 percent.

You think you're busting your butt; you might even be a starter. Seventy-five percent is a solid effort; you feel pretty good about yourself. Hey, there are professional athletes making a 75 percent effort. You'll finish *Train Tough*; it'll make a difference.

A 90 percent want-it rate makes you a player.

Guys look up to you. You've got a few weaknesses that you should be working on. The only question is whether you're going to own up to them or whether you think you're already there. *Train Tough* is a big turn-on. It lights your fire.

Typical Jock: Gee, football season is coming up.
Train Tough Attitude: I've got to recommit to football right now.

Are You 100 Percent? Do You Believe in 110 Percent?

Whether you will give 100 percent effort or better is an important question, because the answer determines how much you're going to get out of the Train Tough strategies. If you're a typical athlete who hovers around a 50 percent effort, you're going to get one thing. If you're a dedicated athlete who's constantly in search of the edge, you're going to get quite another. You get out what you put in.

A 100 percent effort means every fiber of your being is on a mission. You're doing the work; you're positive; you're on task. You accept personal responsibility for your goals and know that reaching them will not be comfortable. You know that the level of dedication that got you where you are is not the level of dedication that will take

---

5 GIVE 110 PERCENT

This level of effort cannot be proven; it exists only as a very powerful idea. It lifts human effort beyond the quantifiable to a whole new level. Imagination is there. Creativity is there. Finding a better way is there. Go there sometime. Soon.

---

6 BE A WARRIOR

Becoming a dedicated athlete is not an easy decision—but it's a choice that leads to extraordinary results. Dedicated athletes are like warriors. Warriors proceed as though the limits of their abilities do not exist. Most athletes try. Warriors don't just try. They perform as though their lives depend on success.

---

you where you want to go. You'll study *Train Tough* and apply the strategies. You want to go for the next level.

At 110 percent we leave planet Earth and enter a whole new realm.

This level of effort cannot be proven; it exists only as a very powerful idea. It lifts human effort beyond the quantifiable to a new level. Imagination is there. Creativity is there. Finding a better way is there.

Players who are 110-percenters read the strategies and say, "Yeah, that's right; that's the way it is." They rise to levels beyond their physical gifts. They don't set out to be anything less than they are capable of being—they want to amaze people.

If they ever do max out, they shift their drive for excellence to something else. They make great coaches, because they've learned all the little things. They've learned how to think, how to sacrifice.

Becoming a dedicated athlete is not an easy decision—but it's a choice that leads to extraordinary results. Dedicated athletes are like warriors. Warriors proceed as though the limits of their abilities do not exist.

Most athletes try. Warriors don't just try—they proceed as if their lives depend on success. There is no try. Warriors give 110 percent and plan on success.

Wanting It

I went to an all-boys boarding school my last two years of high school. Five of us from the school went on to attend Wheaton College outside Chicago after we graduated. Wheaton had the girls. We had the motivation.

Midway through our senior year in prep school we were already plotting how to get in good with the women. We figured most of the freshmen guys would take a wait-and-see attitude. Not us; we were motivated. We knew we had a three-day freshmen orientation, after which the upper classmen would arrive, seriously diminishing our chances for success.

We were up early the first morning of orientation watching the girls go through the cafeteria line. We rated them on a point system. It was like the old Gap Band song used to say—that thing about getting up early in the morning. I always liked that song. There was a man on a mission.

Anyway, 24 hours hadn't gone by before I knew which young lady I was interested in. Actually, "interested in" is an understatement. To me, this young lady was a goddess. But I had a plan. My buddies were great, helping me through my little routines. It's always a plus when guys help each other—you know, beaming each other up, so to speak. It's called teamwork. My future wife never knew what hit her.

> *See if you don't automatically begin acting exactly like a successful athlete acts.*

Thirty years later, we're still together and have brought four great kids onto the planet. I know I reached a little out of my league, but isn't that what it's all about? Where would I be with a wait-and-see attitude? My wife might have found that dentist she was looking for. I don't even want to think about that.

My point?

You've got to want it. *Bad.*

How bad?

When I step up to the plate in baseball I ask myself a simple question: "How bad do you want it?"

There isn't time for a detailed analysis. Sometimes I even have to give myself the benefit of the doubt. It doesn't matter. I give myself a simple answer.

"Bad."

I want it *bad*. Bad enough to get my breathing under control. To heighten my awareness of what the pitcher's throwing. Bad enough to wait for the right pitch and lock on it. Bad enough to smash the ball.

That simple answer provides the focus for success. If you want something bad enough, you find a way to get it. You close off distractions and focus on the task at hand. Your mind is right. Your desire is focused.

The warrior attitude works.

Take on the attitude.

Next time you're bowling, shooting a free throw, getting ready for the high jump, or whatever it is you do, ask yourself, "How bad do I want it?"

Be sure and answer: "*Bad.*"

See if you don't automatically begin acting exactly like a successful athlete acts. See if you don't do exactly what a successful athlete does.

Once you've got the motivational aspect of the task established, the rest is easy. You've been trained to do what's right. And you want to do it real bad. You've got the attitude of the warrior.

Consider the alternative.

We've all seen the ballplayer who pops up with the bases loaded. The bat is flung willy-nilly; the batting helmet is bounced off the turf in disgust. As our hero tears off his batting glove, reality sinks in. An opportunity lost. Only then does he realize how bad he wanted it. If only he'd invested a bit of thought and emotion at the front end of the task, he might have saved himself all the negativity after the task.

An athlete who knows he did everything possible to get the job done copes much better with failure. Failure isn't defeat. In fact, one of the big differences between winners and losers is that losers don't fail enough. They usually quit rather than risk the many little failures that come with sports.

By identifying your level of motivation, you ensure your best effort will come through.

You've got to want it bad.

Journey to Lake Lotawana

U.S. Interstate 70 meanders some two thousand miles across the heartland of America—from Maryland to Utah. Just east of Kansas

---

★ 7 WANT IT BAD

If you want something bad enough, you find a way to get it. You close off distractions and concentrate on the task. Your mind is right. Your desire is focused.

City, about halfway in the journey from either direction, there's an exit sign for Lake Lotawana.

I never pass it without chuckling at the name. It's an Indian word for "sparkling water," but to me it means something totally different. In the language of the warrior it means, "a lot of wanna." When you're in the motivation business, everything speaks to you.

The Lake Lotawana Sailing Club is known throughout the Midwest for overcoming obstacles. The lake is L-shaped with only six hundred acres suitable for sailing. If the wind isn't just right, it's an awkward lake to sail. But the Lotawanians sail anyway. They have the largest junior fleet in the Midwest and one of the few all-women fleets in the country. Their programs start with four-year-olds, whom they place in little boats shaped like bathtubs. It takes a lotawana.

It's a dedication that must be renewed every day, many times throughout the day.

It's New Year's Day, and I've made my own journey to Lake Lotawana. The ice is six inches thick; it's one of the coldest days on record. A solitary iceboat whips around the lake. The ice is good, and I skate with hockey stick in hand, the puck an extension of my mind— a skill developed as a kid on the frozen lakes of Ohio with my dad.

Lotawana. Lotawana. I repeat it to myself as I skate. What a great place for a New Year's resolution.

I vow to play one more year of basketball. Not just to show up, but to excel.

I vow to get my weight back down to 170.

I consecrate myself to a sacred vision—to anticipate success, not fear it. To remain flexible and embrace change. To go after my dreams with a sense of entitlement.

But this high-performance lifestyle will not come as a result of a single dedication. It's a dedication that must be renewed every day, many times throughout the day.

Lotawana. Lotawana.

Does anyone besides the sailing club come to the waters of Lotawana? Do local high school teams come to be baptized before the start of a season?

Isn't there a Lackawanna County in Pennsylvania? Does anything ever get done there?

Lotawana.

I pause at a fishing hole cut into the ice. Removing my glove, I dip my hand into the freezing water and pour the contents over my head. The sparkling water freezes to my face. I've been baptized in the waters of Lake Lotawana.

Lotawana.

This book does more than provide information. It's a vehicle for actual transformation. You'll get information, sure, but more important, I want to transform your mind so you can act on the information. You need to reach down into the freezing water of Lake Lotawana and be baptized into a whole new way of thinking. Yes, you're going to have to want it—*bad*.

TRAIN TOUGH CHALLENGE

- Steer clear of Lackawanna County. It's already overpopulated and a detour you can't afford to take.

- Develop your understanding of motivation in simple tasks. Answer the question, "How bad do I want it?" with a simple response: "Bad."

- How bad do you want it? Assess yourself honestly.

- Commit to the next level. Renew this commitment every day, many times each day.

2

THE COMBAT STANCE

★

Stand erect, or be helped to stand erect. . . . Life is more like wrestling than dancing, in that it should stand ready and firm to meet onsets, however unexpected.
—MARCUS AURELIUS, A.D. 121–180

Wrestling is a lot like life—part opportunity, part threat.

It's a sport requiring mental toughness, strength, quickness, and the drive to keep learning. Those who wrestle just one way go only so far. Somebody builds a better mousetrap.

Every wrestler has a unique stance. Despite the basics of staying low, positioning the hands and arms for control, and protecting the legs, they all set up a little differently. Some wrestlers never get it. You can often tell the winners from the losers by their stance.

Athletes from all sports can learn a lot from wrestling. All sports are part opportunity and part threat. Like a wrestler, you want to be in a position to react quickly to both. You want to be in a combat-ready stance, with a combat-ready attitude.

Loser Mentality: I have my own style, and I'm not going to worry about it.

Train Tough Attitude: I'm fine-tuning a stance that conveys total confidence.

Posturing

Posturing has been given a bad name. And that's too bad. We say someone's posturing when they're projecting an image, sending a message. Teachers posture in the classroom; cops posture on the beat. They both project confidence and authority in the hope that that's all it will take to maintain law and order.

The United States military postures by design. When a situation develops, we want to project strength and readiness—so we might send in a battle carrier group just to show the other guys we mean business. "Are you sure you want some of this?" is what we're saying. We project strength and resolve in the hope that the bad guys will back off.

The first thing a soldier learns when he gets off the bus is how to stand. We want the soldier to project strength, confidence, and uniformity with his peers. The soldier is told to stand up straight, suck in the gut, look straight ahead, and keep a serious expression.

Eye control is very important. We want the soldier to control what he focuses on. At the beginning we want him looking straight ahead in a disciplined manner. Later we might have him looking for bad guys on patrol. Athletes need the same discipline, focusing on the ball and not the cheerleaders.

Then we teach the soldier to march. The soldier doesn't know why we do this, and neither do civilians. It looks kind of stupid, a bunch of soldiers marching around, making themselves easy targets for snipers or a single grenade.

But we know why we're doing it. We're teaching the soldier discipline, pride in the unit, and trust in the leaders. The deal is this—you guys follow my commands, and I'll march you to excellence. The sooner you get it, the sooner we can move on to more important things, like marksmanship and hand-to-hand combat. The soldier is putting trust in the leader. He is learning to project pride, coordination, and teamwork—the same qualities that will be needed in battle.

Eventually, we'll teach the soldier other postures, like how to walk through the jungle. The jungle stance will be different from the parade stance. In the jungle there are only two kinds of soldiers—the quick and the dead. So the soldier will have to be ready for action.

But that comes later. Early on we teach the soldier to take care of the uniform and personal living space. For the kid who was a slob back home, the party's over. Boots are spit-shined, uniforms are pressed and starched, hair is neatly trimmed or just plain sheared. Living quarters are routinely inspected. Rewards and punishments are handed out, reinforcing desired behaviors. Again, we're teaching the soldier to have pride, to project professionalism, to be the kind of soldier that tells the world to watch out—don't mess with Uncle Sam.

> *. . . and when push comes to shove, we have to be ready to shove the hardest.*

We know that maintaining a large, professional Army begins with individual soldiers. If we've taught the soldier well, he will fit in to the organization and make a positive contribution. It can be a life-or-death business, and when push comes to shove, we have to be ready to shove the hardest.

Armies are like teams, and armies keep tabs on each other. The British and Israelis are tough, but on most playing fields the U.S. Army still rules.

One of the untold beauties of Desert Storm was the effect it had on the Chinese. They saw what we could do, and it totally freaked them out. This is a good thing. We want our competitors to have a healthy regard for our capabilities. A bit of posturing and the ability to back it up with force have saved a lot of American lives over the years. Now that our young soldiers are hunting terrorists all over the globe, it's doubly important that they project confidence and professionalism.

The lesson is there for the athlete. That's why your team has uniforms. It's why your sport has a posture and a stance. You always dress for success; your stance is always ready for action.

You Can Always Tell the Pros

One day I'm sitting at the 18th green watching the golfers come in at a local Pro-Am. There's a golfing professional in each foursome, so I figure I'll amuse myself trying to figure out who the pro is in each group.

It turned out to be pretty easy.

Everyone in the tournament was a good golfer, so I couldn't necessarily tell by the drive or second shot. I had to wait until the players approached the green to tell who the pros were.

The pros carried themselves in a different way. They were confident and courteous and radiated leadership—it was clear they were in charge of the group. They had the right grip, the right setup, the right stance over the ball. They were loose and relaxed. Without exception they were well dressed and had the best equipment. They radiated confidence.

The amateurs were generally an impressive group, but they were still amateurs. They took too many practice swings, stood over putts too long. They overreacted to problem situations and showed frustration. Sometimes their attire made them suspect; more often just the way they addressed the ball was a dead giveaway. Every one of them was a big cheese somewhere in life, and all of them were low-handicap golfers. But on the course it didn't take much to separate the men from the boys.

Personal bearing, like military bearing, is something that can be learned. The pros all learn it; that's why they're pros. You have to learn it too—and the sooner the better.

The Matador Walk

This section is not just for bullfighters. It's for every athlete that has to face fear. And guess what? That's all of us.

The matador has a unique challenge. He has to provide entertainment to the crowd, and he has to do it in a life-threatening environment. He's out there to demonstrate courage in the face of adversity. Sure he feels fear—that's what makes the spectacle interesting. But

8 GET IN THE STANCE

In action sports, you want to have that middle linebacker attitude. Get in the stance, Baby. Put your body on the altar of sacrifice and look for something to hit. You're the hitter, not the hittee! Posture and bearing affect thought patterns. Confidence exudes confidence.

he's got an anxiety-management program—he role-plays acting positively, whether he feels like it or not.

The bull is massive, his horns are long and sharp, and he's been tortured. He's looking for something to vent his anger on. A matador would be just fine, thank you.

But the matador stands erect; he walks from place to place with a unique kind of strut. He appears in complete control of the situation. He oozes confidence, assertiveness, freedom from doubt, and certainty in his ability.

Does the matador's strut give him confidence?

Or does his confidence give him the strut?

When the bull charges, the matador deftly pivots out of harm's way. The closer the bull, the more pleasing to the crowd.

Does the matador's stance give him confidence?

Or does his confidence give him the stance?

Posture for Confidence

One day they put me at middle linebacker. Who the genius was who came up with that idea I don't recall. In fact, I don't recall a whole lot from that day. The first two plays resulted in the two hardest hits I ever took on a football field. I never saw them coming; I do remember landing on my butt as the world went by, gasping for air and happy to be alive.

By the third play I realized that if I was going to play linebacker I needed to start acting like one. It was obvious that the wait-and-see strategy wasn't working. I quickly learned to role-play. And it really wasn't that hard. You just get your butt down, get your head up, and start looking for something to kill. That gives you the look. The look gives you the confidence. You feel strong and agile, like a cat. Kill or be killed is a marvelous motivator. Being the hitter is a lot more fun than being the hittee.

Whatever you're doing, you want to have that middle linebacker attitude. Get in the stance, Baby. Put your body on the altar of sacrifice and look for something to hit. If you're wandering around wondering what's going to happen next, you're only making yourself a bad-thing target. You're a hit magnet.

Let me tell you something. There are times when we're all scared silly. It's scary out there, regardless of what sport you're playing. But the issue is not whether we feel fear but how we act in spite of the fear. Used correctly, fear becomes a motivator, a powerful emotion you can harness for peak performance.

There *are* times you have to fake it till you make it. Yours truly at middle linebacker is a classic example. I had no business being there, but, hey, somebody put me in the position so I had to deal with it. I had to get through the fear and take control of the situation.

Remember, you are responsible for how you feel about yourself. Regardless of how bad things get, you decide how to respond. Act positively, whether you feel like it or not. Make it a habit. Your level of achievement is tied to your self-concept. What you think and how you act become self-fulfilling prophecies. In addition to improving your performance, confidence in the face of adversity freaks out your opponents. There's nothing like watching a guy who's down continue

9 HARNESS FEAR

There are times when we're all scared silly. It can be scary out there, regardless of what sport you're playing. But the issue is not whether we feel fear but how we act in spite of the fear. Used correctly, fear becomes a motivator, a powerful emotion you can harness for peak performance. Don't even try to hide from fear—respond to it!

on like nothing happened. Let 'em think you're a little crazy. You've got 'em when they think that.

Get your act together. And sometimes that's what it is—an act. You're acting tough and in control in order to function that way. In most sports you're actually performing only a small percentage of the time. The rest of the time you're either standing around wondering, or you're asserting yourself and getting ready. Get ready.

Look 'em in the eye.
Play the stud.

Place your feet squarely on the ground. Relax. Breathe. Look into a teammate's eyes—feel the confidence.

I'm always amazed when a field-goal kicker isolates himself by standing alone when the other team calls a time-out to ice him. The kicker should be in the huddle, feeling the strength of the team around him. These are the guys who have busted their butts all game to give him a shot at winning it. These are the guys who are going to have to keep the bad guys from blocking the kick. The kicker ought to be drawing on that strength and—yes—feeling of community before he sets up to kick. Then he can emerge from the group to do his thing.

Look 'em in the eye. Play the stud. It rubs off and gets passed around and comes back in an even more powerful form.

What's Your Name?

Get a persona. Develop an attitude. Walk like you know what you're doing. Look people in the eyes. Get yourself a stage name or two.

When I walk on a basketball court, I'm White Michael.

I used to tiptoe out there wondering what was going to happen. Not anymore. I've got my feet on the floor, and I'm cool as a cucumber. I've got gum in my mouth, and I know my man is about to have a bad day. Yeah, I wanna be like Mike.

When it's raining jumpers I'm World B. Free. That's right, Lloyd World B. Free. Pleased to meetcha.

Volleyball? I'm Kevin Bashnagel. I'm here to bash the ball.

10 GET YOUR ACT TOGETHER

And sometimes that's what it is—an act. You're acting tough and in control in order to function that way. In most sports you're actually performing only a small percentage of the time. The rest of the time you're either standing around wondering, or you're asserting yourself and getting ready. Get ready. After you've played tough for a couple of outings, you'll realize something very important—you're tougher than woodpecker lips.

You get the idea.

To have confidence, you've got to show confidence. Put the combat stance on whatever you're doing. Make it a habit. Heck, people can tell I'm a military man when I'm on a dance floor. The Army taught me how to stand up straight, how to look like somebody. Now it's a habit.

Make your own habits. Develop your own stance. Get ready.

What's *your* name?

TRAIN TOUGH CHALLENGE

- Be ready. Your stance must allow you to react to both challenge and opportunity.

- Watch the pros; then act like one.

- Remember the matador—even in a life-or-death situation, he oozes confidence.

- How tough are you, really? Pretty tough? Then make that part of your persona.

3

DESERVE TO WIN

★

In war, you win or lose, live or die—and the difference is just an eyelash.

— GENERAL DOUGLAS MACARTHUR

The culture today is fascinated with no-effort strategies. It's wonderful; all we have to do is invest in the right stocks and we'll never have to work again. All we need is the right vacuum cleaner and housework will be a breeze. With the right computer software we'll know everything all the time.

There's a tremendous demand for no-effort solutions. There are no-effort diets, no-effort exercise machines—even no-effort sports psychologies.

I saw a golf film recently extolling the virtues of relaxation and visualization, claiming the process could take 10 strokes off your handicap in a weekend. Some of the mental techniques were right on, but the models they had demonstrating the shots were 50-handicappers! Of course you can drop 10 strokes when you're that bad. Nowhere in the film were the proper golf techniques even mentioned. Practice was an alien concept. Worse, the viewer was treated to an hour of lousy golfers butchering the fundamentals. The message to me was mind over matter, mind over fundamentals, mind over everything.

It doesn't work that way. If it did, we could all walk out on the course and easily master the task with a few mental cues. Anybody who's played golf knows it doesn't work that way. It's going to take some effort.

Not Bad: May the best person win.
Train Tough Attitude: That would be me. I did the work.

Everybody Wants It on Game Day

Suppose you're playing in the company golf tournament. Would you like to do well? Of course you would. Everyone who shows up would like to do well. Nobody shows up thinking, "Gee, I sure hope I can stink the place out."

The fact is, you'll pretty much get what you deserve. If you have no idea about the technique for hitting the ball out of a sand trap, sand traps are almost certainly going to be a problem for you. If you show up at the last second and rush to the first tee, you really don't deserve to hit a screamer down the middle.

There is something to be said for beginner's luck and the occasional mind-clearing phenomenon of an "I didn't have time to think about it" drive. Sometimes you play your best golf after you've been away from the game for a while.

11 DO THE WORK

The most direct route to the deserve-it mentality is to do the work. Teams that are honestly convinced that they have worked harder and smarter than the competition can also be convinced that they deserve to win. They're more invested. When they see that their investment is larger, they realize that the stakes are greater for them. They have more to lose; they gain more by winning.

But the point is that winning the company golf tournament will take effort. It will take lessons, practice, and previous competitions under similar conditions. It will take strategic design—a plan to build a deep base of technique and experience that affords the best chance of success. It will take "wanting it" in practice and the will to make every effort count toward the big day.

Ultimately, you want to be able to walk on the course and say, "You know what, I *deserve* to win this golf tournament."

We Did the Work

I always enjoy the role of player-coach. To me it's the ultimate challenge—strategizing for the whole team while having to set a personal example on the field or court. I'm not standing behind the team yelling, "Charge!" I'm out in front saying, "Follow me." One of my main missions as the leader is to convince my team that we deserve to win. I convince my team of a simple statement: we deserve it more than they do.

> *Discipline is doing what needs to be done, when it needs to be done, and doing it the right way every time.*

The most direct route to the deserve-it mentality is to do the work. Teams that are honestly convinced that they have worked harder and smarter than the competition can also be convinced that they deserve to win. They're more invested. When they see that their investment is larger, they realize that the stakes are greater for them. They have more to lose; they gain more by winning.

Teams and individual players need goals. Then they need to ask the question, "What will it take to achieve the goals?" The answer always involves a tremendous amount of work. If it doesn't, then the goals aren't high enough. Lofty goals have high requirements.

I want my teams to use every minute of practice time to maximum advantage. There is no standing around, no halfhearted efforts. Every goof-up is dissected and analyzed. Every good thing is applauded and reinforced. Every effort is directed toward success in the game. I want my players to take a message from practice: this guy knows what he's doing. He will not accept a low-effort practice performance.

12 SET HIGH GOALS

Teams and individual players need goals. Then they need to ask the question, "What will it take to achieve the goals?" The answer always involves a tremendous amount of work. If it doesn't, then the goals aren't high enough. Lofty goals have high requirements.

My goal is to have a superior training plan that enforces systematic effort. If we take shortcuts it's because we have to. We never take shortcuts unless we know why. Time is always a factor—wasted practice time can't be recovered.

I want disciplined teams. Discipline is doing what needs to be done, when it needs to be done, and doing it the right way every time. I explain the discipline, the lifestyle, and the level of commitment.

As a player you need to convince yourself that it's worth it, and then do the work. My personal motivation isn't trophies or glory; it is simply winning, because it's there.

Get Over the Fear of Success

Satan has a younger brother; I call him Sadon. Like many brothers, the two are a lot alike. Satan's the meaner hombre of the two, but Sadon is no pushover.

Sadon manages the fear-of-success department. He likes nothing more than hearing you whisper to yourself, way down in your subconscious, "I don't deserve it. I'm not good enough."

We all wrestle with Sadon. He can wreak havoc with your self-esteem. He wants to take you on a guilt trip. And while you're away, you'll be getting your butt kicked.

There are a couple of ways to keep him off your back.

First, ask yourself what's really going on. What is making you fear success? Is it a sibling thing? Sadon's the master of sibling relationships, and he's a real bear for the younger ones. The first one out of the chute gets to set the agenda, while the younger brothers and sisters have to grow around the shadow that's cast. Even if the younger ones are more talented, they have a tough time beating big brother or sister. The older ones think they deserve to rule, and the younger ones tend to agree. When push comes to shove, seniority is a huge psychological advantage.

Watching the Williams sisters on the tennis courts has provided a classic example. Serena, the younger of the two, has been a better tennis player for a couple of years now. But, until recently, she just wasn't able to climb the psychological hill to beat big sister Venus. They both said "it's just another match" when they played each other, but we all knew it wasn't. It was sibling rivalry at its finest. As

Understand the challenge.

hard as it was for Serena to lose, it was a lot harder for Venus when her turn came. For a while, Sadon was having a ball with Serena. She finally had to whip him—and Venus.

What else might be causing fear of success? Is it a self-worth thing? A failure to fully invest in the quest? Understand the challenge.

Second, if something makes you feel guilty, stop doing it. For example, if you're cheating yourself and your team by using drugs or binge drinking, listen to the guilt and knock it off. Obey your conscience when it sounds reasonable.

Third, accept your imperfections. When your expectations are unreasonable, it's easy to become frustrated and negetive. Nobody's perfect, and nobody should expect to be. It's not about perfection, it's about achieving excellence in the face of our imperfections.

Finally, there's always professional help. Just don't say anything about Sadon.

Think of Winning as Something That Is Yours

Take two guys in a knock-down, drag-out fight. It's one kind of fight in the street, a neutral site. It's a completely different fight when a guy is defending his home from an intruder. The latter guy will fight with a completely different attitude; he's fighting on his own turf, defending his home. He may feel justified in using deadly force; he knows the law is in his corner in a way it wouldn't be in the street. He's absolutely convinced that he deserves to win.

Every spring we see the same thing in the skies here in Missouri—little birds chasing big birds. The big birds come to steal the young of the little birds, and the little birds don't like that. The little birds get fired up and just chase the big birds all the way to the Kansas state line and halfway to Lawrence.

Find a way to think of yourself as the little bird, mad enough to chase the bigger bird into the next state. You deserve to raise your young. You're not going to put up with seeing them carried off by another bird—no matter how big—and having them be gobbled up.

Or think of it this way: it's your apartment. Somebody's stealing your stuff, and now they're going to fight you for it? I don't think so.

Deserve to win.

Total Commitment

I joined the Army in the mid-'70s, a goofball time to be in. The Army was regrouping from the psychological blow of Vietnam, and the country was recovering from the Nixon resignation, getting primed for the Jimmy Carter malaise. It was a funky time to be an American.

The Army was a huge, unknown object to me—something I wasn't very sure about. It took a while to acclimate and to realize I was part of the greatest organization on the face of the Earth. In those days it was just a paycheck and a chance to play four team sports a year.

Into this mix came a young battalion commander with a different view of the world. His motto was "total commitment," and he expected us to greet each other with this spirited refrain whenever military courtesy dictated a salute.

We thought he was crazy. Most of us weren't even partially committed, and "totally" was an expression for surfers.

Last time I checked, my old commander was a three-star general.

And you know what?

He deserves it.

We may not have bought into total commitment, but he did.

Total commitment is more than a slogan; it's a way of life, a goal. It's something to aspire to. It is key to the deserve-to-win philosophy. When you're totally committed, you can't help but believe you deserve to win.

Total commitment means you've thoroughly prepared. You've done all the work, and done it smart, following a strategic plan with the goal of achieving victory. You've thought through all the obstacles, including the unexpected ones. You won't be surprised to be surprised. You expect adversity—heck, you crave it.

You're motivated. In the military we like to call a guy "highly motivated"—it has a nice ring. You're externally motivated by the need for pig iron (trophies) and the glory and acclaim that come with victory. More important, you're internally motivated by the need to win, simply because it's there. You're motivated. You are highly motivated.

Your motivation is intense. It's a burning sensation, the urge to get it on.

Your motivation is directed. It's directed at whatever it takes to win, whether it's reaching for a backhand, putting a serve in, or putting an overhead away. You've been this way from the very beginning, way back when you first started practicing—every move was made with the goal of victory in mind. That's why you deserve to win.

You've outworked your opponent. You're better prepared. You passed on that cheeseburger and fries two hours before match time. You showed up hungry. You knew it would be two dogs fighting for a bone. The hungriest dog wins.

There's no question. You deserve it.

TRAIN TOUGH CHALLENGE

- Commit to do the work necessary to win.

- Don't accept low-effort performance in yourself or your teammates.

- Watch out for Sadon—the little voice that lies, saying, "You're not good enough."

- Remember, when you're totally committed, you can't help but feel you deserve to win.

4

SCHOOL OF THE SOLDIER

$$\star$$

Training prepares soldiers, leaders, and units to fight and win in war—the Army's basic mission. Training is the Army's top priority and don't you forget it!
—GENERAL CARL VUONO, FROM ARMY FIELD MANUAL 25-101, BATTLE FOCUSED TRAINING

When coaches are asked to choose between two similar athletes, one with a tad more physical ability or one with a tad more smarts, they all take the athlete with smarts. They want the player who's the better learner. Let's make sure that player is you.

> **Tired Thinking:** I'll get it eventually. At least I'm ahead of Tony over there.
> **Train Tough Attitude:** I gotta rub this stuff in—like my life depends on it!

College of the Soldier

Welcome to the Combat University. You do your own work here and take your own tests. You can cheat only yourself.

You do your own thinking here, your own experiments. There are no nifty spaces for you to write in. Find your own places to write.

It's a lifelong course, and you need to think of yourself as a lifelong learner. But the object is to learn fast and learn early. You're always looking to graduate to the next level.

We try not to take things too seriously here at the college. We try to remember that it's only a game and that we're lucky to be playing. We laugh in the face of death.

Accept Where You Are—and Learn from There

The Combat Maneuver Training Center in Hohenfels, Germany, is one of the toughest learning environments on Earth. When it's dry, it's a dust bowl; when it rains, it's an instant mud hole.

U.S. Army combat battalions spend a week there every year, fighting a "home team" opposing force that is well practiced and almost impossible to beat. Both sides fire lasers at each other. If you can't shoot straight, you find out what it's like to die. It's as close to the real thing as I ever want to get.

When the battle's over it gets worse. That's when the "after-action review," or "AAR," begins. The key players gather in a high-tech auditorium for a "guided discussion" of how things went. Some people call it a bloodletting session. It certainly feels that way.

There are a lot of athletes out there in denial about their game.

Nothing ever goes according to plan in combat. You need a plan, but you have to be able to adjust. The enemy's there to screw you up. The AAR is there to show you how you did and what you need to work on for next time.

There's no place to hide. All the radio traffic is recorded, so if you try to bull your way out of something, they just play back the tape. You say you weren't sleeping on perimeter guard? Here's film of enemy tanks rolling right by your position while you never fired a shot.

There's no whining allowed. If you sucked, you sucked. Better to find out now than on the battlefield. Armies that lie to themselves get smoked in war. The truth hurts, but not nearly as badly as a bullet. One brigade commander liked to end discussion with the statement, "Accept it. Just accept it."

The analogy holds true in sports. You've got to know where you stand and accept where you are. If you stink, you stink. Admitting it is the first step. Then you can do something about it. There are a lot of athletes out there in denial about their game. They think they're team players, but they're not. They think they're playing defense, but they aren't.

When somebody points out a problem or a weakness you have, accept it. Be open. Be coachable. Don't take it personally. Getting defensive is taking a step away from the reality you need to confront.

The truth eventually comes out in the sporting world—usually during the game. Get it out before then, so you can learn from it.

Learn Early, Learn Fast, Learn *Now*

Last week I got a call from Antoine, an old acquaintance. He needed someone to fill in on his volleyball team. The last time I played volleyball with Antoine was 20 years ago in a regional tournament in California. I was a little hesitant to try it again. He had been an inconsistent player, an underachiever. At six feet, four inches he had the perfect volleyball build, and he always looked great in warm-ups. But when the whistle blew he was largely in the way.

Tiger Woods is a great example of what to shoot for.

Not anymore. Now in his forties, Antoine played like a commando. Solid as a rock. He didn't have the same spring, but he more than made up for it with a new competitiveness and consistent execution of fundamentals.

I wondered—"When in the past 20 years did the light turn on? When did Antoine finally get it? How far out of his prime was he?"

I'm not picking on Antoine. I put myself in the same category—a late bloomer. But how much better would it have been to learn the lessons early, to have the knowledge along with the juice of youth?

Tiger Woods is a great example of what to shoot for. There are films of Tiger swinging a golf club at age three. At every level he's ahead of the pack. Now he dominates the professional tour in his physical prime. He is always learning, so even as he ages, he'll dominate with skills and experience.

Get there early. Start now.

Commit to Learning

Learning is a commitment. Knowledge and new skills do not just rub off on you because you happen to be in a classroom or gym. You have to rub them in, and that takes energy and dedication. For most of us, it's painful. Too bad—you've got to take the pain. After a while, if you stick with it, it gets easier. It becomes a habit.

Take responsibility for your own learning. Don't lay it on the coach. Don't expect it to just happen. You've got to make it happen. Rise above the excuses that it's boring or it won't work. Make it work.

Who learns more in a conversation between a wise man and a fool? Most people say the fool because he's got so much to learn, and the wise man already knows so much. Most people are dead wrong.

13 COMMIT TO LEARNING

Learning is a commitment. Knowledge and new skills do not just rub off on you because you happen to be in a classroom or gym. You have to rub them in, and that takes energy and dedication. For most of us, it's painful. Too bad—you've got to take the pain. After a while, if you stick with it, it gets easier. It becomes a habit. Take responsibility for your own learning. Don't lay it on the coach. Don't expect it to just happen. You've got to make it happen. Rise above the excuses that it's boring or it won't work. Make it work.

The fool never learns. He thinks he knows it all.

The wise man is always learning. He can learn even from a fool.

Most of learning is attitude. If you think you're too stupid, you are. If you think you can handle it, you can. Develop confidence. You may not be the brightest light in the gym ceiling, but you can make up for that with extra effort and attitude. How many of your team-

> *You want to be playing with the big kids, not the little kids.*

mates have ever looked at the rule book? Have you? A quick look at the rule book would put you ahead of 99 percent of the players in your sport who've never even seen the thing. How hard is that?

Learn How *You* Learn

We all have preferences for how we learn. Some like to read, some like to observe, and some are excellent listeners. Some people have to experience the task before it sinks in. How do you learn? Would you rather read, observe, listen, or experience?

You must be able to do all four. If you're weak in an area, you need to work on it. The world is not going to reinvent itself according to your desires. Identify your weaknesses and work on them.

Observing

The greatest-observer-of-all-time award goes to the guy with the Navy binoculars, my dad. Ask for a major league batting stance or a PGA tour golf swing, and he can give it to you, on the spot. Ted Williams, Mark McGwire, Mickey Mantle, Jack Nicklaus, Arnold Palmer, Tiger Woods—he can show you them all. He can do the physical piece, the mannerisms, and the attitude. He can do the grip, the follow-through, and the personality.

How does he do it? He's learned to observe. He doesn't just go to the ballpark or watch a golf tournament on TV. He observes. He looks for the nuances. He can tell when a guy's going to sink a putt or is serious about hitting a baseball.

Bobby Richardson, a family friend and six-time Gold Glove winner with the New York Yankees, used to hide behind the watercooler between innings. My dad had mentioned to him that he'd noticed him adjusting his jockstrap on the bench. Bobby realized his every move was under study.

Make yourself an observer. Notice things. Take advantage of the video revolution to tape yourself, your opponents, and the fundamentally sound players to review and study.

Next time you're in the gym, look at the wrist action on the various jump shots. Observe the footwork. Take notes. Make observation a habit.

Listening

I was never a very good listener, and I've paid a tremendous price in effectiveness as a result. I don't want the same thing to happen to you. So listen up.

You've got to listen with more than your ears. That's just hearing. Listening is using your mind. It's digesting and storing what you hear and then being able to retrieve it when it counts. That takes effort.

Your body language tells the tale. Do you appear alert? What's your posture? Are you up front hanging on every word, or are you hiding in the back?

A good listener is listening with his eyes, giving off some sparkle. The head nods in agreement or tilts slightly when something's not clear. A good listener gives feedback and has questions. Listening is not a passive experience; it's an activity. I want you to be an active listener.

You must be open to listening. When I was 12 my father told me I was too tight shooting the basketball, that I needed to loosen up. Like most kids that age I wasn't open to suggestion from a parent. I heard what he said, but I didn't listen. As a result I spent a lot of years in the wilderness as a mediocre shooter—a good playmaker, yes, but an inconsistent shooter. It wasn't until five years ago that I discovered for myself what Dad meant. Now I've got a deadly jumper—but it's too bad I went so long without it.

Reading

I was a lousy math student in school. It wasn't until I taught myself statistics from a programmed text that I realized I was OK in math as long as I could read about it and didn't have to try and follow a teacher. Reading is my preferred way of learning.

That's not the case for most athletes, which helps explain why many athletes can learn the complexities of their sport and still be lousy students in the classroom. As a group we're lousy readers. Most of us don't know that there are different ways of reading.

A little while back I suggested you take a "quick look" at the rule book. Many of you immediately dismissed that idea because you don't know what I meant by a "quick look." Right away you imagined yourself bogged down at the front end of a rule book. Boring.

That's not what I meant. I meant a look-see at the table of contents and some skimming, just to get the feel of the thing. If you find something interesting, you read it—"Wow. Didn't know you can't punch the basketball with your fist."—that kind of thing. Five minutes. Max.

Reading is a helpful skill for athletes, but it's a critical life skill.

Experiencing

Ultimately, you've got to experience performing in the arena . . . in game situations. There are some things you can learn no other way. You want to put yourself in situations where you can learn—places where you're surrounded by the best possible talent, coaching, and facilities. You want to be playing with the big kids, not the little kids. You need to get knocked on your butt so you can figure out how to get back up.

Norman, my neighbor, is into demolition derby. He's an excellent mechanic and just crazy enough to be right for the sport. He did his first derby last summer. Being out there opened up a whole new world for him. "I really had no idea what it would be like," he said, "sheer terror. I was driving around in circles getting creamed. Next year it's up and back, up and back—until it breaks."

Some things you just have to experience to understand.

Know *What* to Learn

You've got to know *how* to learn; you must also know *what* to learn. Some of these things seem intuitively obvious, yet it's amazing how many athletes stagger around not really sure what to pay attention to. Here are the big five.

Fundamentals

The soldier who doesn't master the skill of his weapon dies early. Players who take a shortcut through the fundamentals go only so far. Then they have to come back and do the work, and often it's too late. Focus on fundamentals early; rub 'em in.

Learn the language of your sport. Tex Winter, the inventor of basketball's triangle offense, had a name for various situations. Rather than numbering plays, he named things—like "wing quickie," "dribble weave," and "center rub." He can mention "button hook" to a player he coached 50 years ago, and the guy will know exactly what he's talking about.

Teamwork

You've got to learn the team plays—the Xs and Os that go with the sport you play. For many of us, that's difficult. We've learned to rely on our individual skill and improvisation to get by. But that's a narrow view of the situation. How much better would it be to be the master of the team system?

The key to mastery is learn as you go. Learn the stuff while the coach is taking you through it instead of telling yourself you'll learn it later. That's the "learn now" strategy—never put off until later what you can learn right now.

Become a learning machine. When you've mastered the team concept you'll be freed up to maximize your individual skill and to improvise—instead of using those skills to merely catch up.

Conditioning

You need to know what it takes to be in shape for your sport, including the little extras that make a difference. You also need to know the level of dedication it will take to get there. You need to learn how to motivate yourself.

Nobody can get you in shape but you. In the Army we have physical training three times a week. There's a lot of focus on push-ups, sit-ups, and the two-mile run. These are the things we test for every six months. Despite the mandatory training, there are soldiers who never improve. They're spending the time just going through the motions. It's hard to be working out and not get any better, but some guys find a way. Don't be like that.

Focus

Learn how to get control of your mind, to keep it on task. You've got to master fear, self-consciousness, apprehension, and distraction. Every one of those is a 10-foot giant that you must learn to deal with.

You must learn to stay "in the moment." That means focusing on task and not worrying about result. It's a tough challenge. But if you apply the Train Tough strategies, you can do it.

Can you imagine yourself being successful? Sinking putts? Hitting jump shots?

Players who have difficulty with a task often have the same difficulty even imagining doing it right. You have to believe you can do it in order to visualize doing it. Then you can rehearse being successful through some simple visualization techniques.

Sometimes an athlete needs to think differently about a task. Visualization can help.

A few years ago I was an instructor at the Army's premier problem-solving course for young officers. Among other tortures, the captains had to play volleyball—the perfect sport for team building. Over time we found that about a third of the captains were athletic, a third were coachable, and a third were just plain clumsy. You never knew what kind of mix you'd wind up with.

One team I had was loaded with clumsies. They couldn't get it through their heads that they needed to stay alert, keep their knees bent with eyes on the ball, and move quickly to get into optimal position to control the ball. This group wanted to just reach out and swipe at it. The ball was killing us. Then I asked them a couple of questions: "What if the ball were a baby coming over the net? Is that how you'd move to save it?"

I answered the question for them as I demonstrated: "No, you'd lock your eyes on the baby and you'd move quickly to save it. You'd move with your butt low, using your legs as shock absorbers. Your entire being would be motivated to save the baby. In short, you'd be doing everything you're supposed to be doing to bump a volleyball."

A baby was something they could visualize. Saving a baby was something that got them focused and moving.

Resiliency

One of the tough lessons of sport is defeat. It comes in many packages. It can mean being beaten on a single play, losing a game, or tanking a season. It can come in the form of injury or a team roster without your name on it. By design, sport is not all sweetness and light. Obstacles, setbacks, and losses are part of the challenge.

It's designed to make you want to quit—either by walking off the field or, more insidiously, by quitting a little bit at a time.

---

14 BE COACHABLE

When somebody points out a problem or a weakness you have, accept it. Be open. Be coachable. Don't take it personally. Getting defensive is taking a step away from the reality you need to confront. The truth eventually comes out in the sporting world—usually during the game. Get it out before then, so you can learn from it.

Learn what it takes to stay in the game, to dust yourself off and ask for more. The fiercest opponent is the one who never quits, who never lets up.

You can and must learn from defeat. More important, you must learn how to turn what appear to be defeats into victories.

Look for Mentors

Mentors are older, more experienced hands who are willing to point the way. They have to be willing to share, and you have to be willing to listen—and then act. Mentors see things that you can only guess at. They see because they've been there, both in victory and in defeat. They know the way.

Is there someone you know who can guide you to the next level?

Sometimes a mentor can open doors for you, introduce you to the right people. So choose your mentors as you would choose a brain surgeon. Learn the difference between someone who wants to help and someone who really can be helpful.

I was lucky. Because my dad was involved with pro athletes, I had three mentors growing up that taught me valuable lessons.

Bobby Richardson of the New York Yankees played in eight World Series. He taught me that you can be fiercely competitive and still demonstrate character.

Bill Glass, All-Pro defensive end for the World Champion Cleveland Browns, taught me the value of visualization. He used psychocybernetics to prepare for every game. It gave him a calm before the storm of the utter abandon with which he played.

Bobby Murcer, All-Star outfielder with the New York Yankees, was the older brother I never had. He carried himself with the bearing of a warrior, and nobody was better in the clutch. There was a toughness about Bobby that was matched only by the supreme confidence he exuded.

Richardson took me to Yankees tryouts. Glass took me to Browns team meetings. Murcer and I used to go one-on-one in basketball. They showed me things and took me places I would never have experienced without them.

Is there someone you know who can guide you to the next level? Think about it as we continue the quest.

TRAIN TOUGH CHALLENGE

Learn how to learn. Figure out what you don't know and get to work on it. You've got to commit to learning and growing—and it's a tough job. Observe. Listen. Read. Perform. That's how you learn.

Remember the big five areas an athlete needs to master:

1. Fundamentals
2. Teamwork
3. Conditioning
4. Focus
5. Resiliency

Then find a mentor—someone who knows the way and can pull while you push your way up.

PART TWO

THE COMBAT TEAM
HOW TO MAKE IT,
HOW TO LEAD IT

5

YOU'RE ALWAYS TRYING OUT

★

In the real world, I'll bet that six of my twenty-four rookies this year will fall away for lack of conditioning. And that another seven or eight will be cut for not knowing what to do. And that another handful will prove undependable.

—Bill Parcells

Not making the baseball team at West Point was one of the greatest disappointments of my life, maybe the greatest.

—General Dwight Eisenhower,
34th president of the United States

Once upon a time, a long, long time ago, I player-coached an international softball team called the AFCENT Knights. AFCENT stood for Allied Forces Central Europe. We were the guys who would have directed the main land battle in Europe if the Soviets attacked. Along with prepping for that awesome event, we played a lot of softball. We traveled around by bus, terrorizing the other military teams in Europe.

One spring a tremendous buzz developed about a gigantic military policeman who was said to be jacking the ball into the ionosphere. He was an impressive guy but had arrived in country too late to try out for the team. I didn't want to have to cut another guy to pick him up, and I wasn't sure how he'd fit in. His name was Jack Lamey.

The next thing I know, Lamey rounded up some scrubs and wanted to take on the Knights. It was early in the season so we figured we'd get together for a practice game.

By the end of the game I was begging Jack Lamey to become a Knight.

All things being equal, a player who plays the tryout game will get picked up over a player who doesn't.

His ragtag group beat us pretty good that day, but what really shook me up was Lamey himself. There was blood in his eye. He had *the look*. I was pitching, so I got a good view of the ball leaving the ballpark. Jack could absolutely crush a softball. He was out to show me what he could do—and he did.

Jack Lamey was the real deal, the MacDaddy of sluggers. He maintained that same intensity for the two seasons we were together. There was no one I'd rather have at the plate with the game on the line than Jack Lamey. He was always trying out.

Loser Mentality: Coach doesn't like me.
Train Tough Attitude: Coach is gonna love the way I play ball.

Do the Work—and Be Sure and Show Up

Actor and director Woody Allen once said, "Ninety percent of success is just showing up." Woody was right—even though it's hard to imagine him running with a football.

A lot of guys could make a team, but for one reason or another, they never show up to try out. Usually it's because of a fear of failure.

Make a commitment to showing up, then get to work preparing to try out.

It makes no sense to show up for a tryout in less than your best playing form. The guidelines in this chapter are all predicated on the assumption that you did the work necessary to get on top of your game for tryouts. Tryouts are not the time to be getting back into the swing of things.

And guess what? You can't cram for tryouts like you might for a world history test. There are no multiple-choice questions. You've got to prepare over time. Tryouts are where the planned approach pays off. You show up in top shape, having honed your fundamentals. Then you've got a chance.

The other thing you want to do is get inside the system early. Get to know the coaches. Ask them questions. Try and figure out their approach to the season. Be seen working out. Find out what the team studs are doing and, if they're doing the right things, do those things with them.

And let's face it, some guys are going to make the team regardless of tryouts. They may not even have to try out—they're already on the team. Kobe Bryant is not going to be trying out for the Los Angeles Lakers next season. But there was a time when Kobe tried out, and if he stays around long enough he'll have to try out again. Sooner or later we all find ourselves on the bubble. The bubble is where little things spell the difference between making a team and getting cut—between establishing yourself as a player and relegating yourself to the bench.

This chapter assumes you've done the work. It's written for those who are on the bubble—struggling to make a team, or an impression. All things being equal, a player who plays the tryout game will get

15 PREPARE OVER TIME

You can't cram for tryouts like you might for a world history exam. There are no multiple-choice questions. You've got to prepare over time. Tryouts are where the planned approach pays off. Show up in top shape, having honed your fundamentals. Then you've got a chance.

picked up over a player who doesn't. But it only goes so far. Some coaches will pick up players with police records, drug problems, and bad attitudes if they think the guys have the talent to help the team.

The guys with talent are going to make the team. The guys with no talent are not going to make the team. On the bubble are a bunch of players who could go either way. This chapter is written for them.

What Coaches Want

In the Army everybody changes jobs and locations every two or three years. The average time you work for a boss is a year. In that time you've got to figure out what the boss really wants, and then try to give it to him. In every unit there's a cottage industry of simply trying to figure out what the boss wants. Sometimes the boss will actually tell you what he wants, but you have to be careful, it may not be

> *Whether they admit to it or not, all coaches are influenced by politics.*

what he *really* wants. After a while soldiers get pretty good at cutting through the bull and focusing on accomplishing the things that are important.

Figuring out a coach is much the same. What kind of animal is the coach? What gets emphasized? What kind of players were chosen in the past?

Most coaches ask Bill Parcells–type questions when evaluating a player: Does the player have the physical skills? Has he mastered the fundamentals? Can he learn our system? What has he done in the past? Is he a team player? How tough is he? Does he cause trouble?

Assess yourself the same way a coach does. Then show him a player that has the skills, fundamentals, coachability, toughness, and dedication to teamwork that are required. In fact, aim to exceed standards. What would it take to amaze the coaching staff?

Sometimes you make a team because you get caught doing something good. You need to be performing when it counts.

Some tryouts are very quantified. Performance is measured objectively and decisions are influenced by how a player scores over a range of mostly physical skills. Other tryouts are largely subjective, with the coaches watching and observing and going with their gut instincts. Either way, the answers to the previous questions largely determine whether or not you make the team. Except for one thing: politics.

Whether they admit to it or not, all coaches are influenced by politics.

Remember how the coach's kid always got to play in Little League? And how the assistant coach's kid was next in line? In college the athletes with scholarships have an advantage. The coach wants to feel good about recruited players in particular. In the pros it's the players with the big signing bonuses or the big salaries, especially if the incumbent coaching staff is invested in their success. That's politics. And guess what? If you're on the bubble, you can't afford not to play.

Dress for success. Show up on time, preferably ahead of time. Demonstrate character. Make the right friends.

If you're pals with players who are going to get cut, you're probably going with them. You might as well be pals with the ones who are going to make it. Most teams have cliques, and you might want to be in with the in crowd. If I played for the Lakers, I'd want to be tight with Shaq.

Where Can You Fit In?

And whom do you have to beat out?

Early on in tryouts you want to be sizing up the competition, figuring what you have to do to stay ahead of it. If Johnny just ran the 40-yard dash in 4.5, you want to be aiming for 4.4. If you can't beat

---

16 BE VERSATILE

Demonstrate versatility. Be a guy who can play anywhere; it gives the coach more options for keeping you.

him in the 40, you better be demonstrating that you can make the right decisions, even if Johnny is a step faster.

Don't be too easily impressed with the glamour boys, even if they're studs. The coaching staff is looking for guys who can hang with the top players. Stand up to those guys. Put your best game on them.

Demonstrate versatility. You may want to play wide receiver, but if you can't make it there, can you play cornerback? Special teams? Be a guy that can play anywhere; it gives the coach more options for keeping you.

> *Be a guy that can play anywhere; it gives the coach more options for keeping you.*

What things can you do to help the team win? Can you bunt? Steal? Put on the gear and go behind the plate to catch? Maybe you like to work with pitchers and won't mind catching for them in warm-ups. You're already more valuable than a guy who's stuck in one position and plays only one kind of game.

Figure out the chemistry of the team and fit in.

If you do get cut, don't burn any bridges. Tell the coach you're available if he changes his mind or the team needs you later.

There are also situations where, for whatever reason, you're just not going to fit in. Hey, it happens. Frankly, it happens a lot. My advice in that situation is to move on. Do whatever's reasonable to find another operation where your game will be appreciated—and learn from the experience.

It might even be time to change sports.

When my son Bob couldn't get around on the fastball in Little League, we moved on and concentrated on soccer. When he was 10 he went through an entire basketball season without taking a shot. It was obvious it was time to go back to wrestling—where he eventually competed at state level.

Trying out is a good thing, even in failure. The operative word is *trying*. It shows initiative, the same stuff you need in life.

That's why I say, you're always trying out.

TRAIN TOUGH CHALLENGE

- Get ready for tryouts, *now*.

- Get inside the system. Figure out the coach. Make the right pals.

- Identify some places you can fit in. Demonstrate *versatility*.

- If you get cut, move on. Find a place or a sport where you fit. And don't burn any bridges.

6

PRACTICE—AND THE ART OF THE BATTLE DRILL

★

Challenging training inspires excellence by fostering initiative, enthusiasm, confidence, and the ability to apply the learned tasks in the dynamic environment of combat.
—FROM ARMY FIELD MANUAL 25-101,
BATTLE FOCUSED TRAINING

My son Matt and I saw the Chiefs and the Chargers play at Arrowhead Stadium recently. I try not to get too wrapped up in spectator sports, but we were like two dogs going hunting just driving to the stadium.

Naturally, we got there early, in time to watch the teams warm up. And warm-ups were all it took to see who came to play. It wasn't the San Diego Chargers. Not on this day, anyway. The Chargers receivers were practicing dropping the ball. The ones they didn't drop, they bobbled. And guess what? That's exactly what they did in the game.

The Chargers got off to a 10–0 lead and then collapsed in a 42–10 rout.

A big part of their problem was dropped balls. They performed exactly like they practiced in warm-ups.

There's a direct relationship between practice and performance. How you practice affects how you perform. If you slack off in practice, you get paid back during the game. If you have poorly designed practices, you've wasted precious time and energy.

The will to win begins with the will to prepare. And that means dynamic, focused practice.

Typical Jock Mentality: This is boring.

Train Tough Attitude: We're getting this down to a science.

What Combat Units Learn About Practice

Preparing for war is a serious business. With the millions of distractions of life in the Army's vast bureaucracy, it's easy for a combat unit to lose focus. Bad things happen when they do. One day the commander wakes up and realizes that not only can his soldiers no longer shoot straight but they are unpracticed in the more complex tasks they must accomplish on the battlefield. It's a constant battle to keep a unit trained and ready to go.

You don't want to send your field-goal unit out on the field with the feeling that "we'll see what happens."

One of the commander's tools is the Mission Essential Task List, or METL. The METL consists of the no-fooling six or seven battlefield tasks his unit *must* be able to accomplish in order to be successful on the battlefield.

For example, every unit must be able to deploy. That means they've got to be able to get from where they are to the battlefield. It's not as easy as it sounds. Every soldier must be individually ready. He must be physically fit for combat, have his will and power of attorney up to date, and have his family taken care of. He's got to have all his gear. The commander verifies that each soldier is ready to go.

The unit's got to move its weapons, vehicles, and equipment. They've got to know how to convoy, load up their ammunition, travel, and then move into battlefield positions in a constant state of alert. A glitch here or there can really screw things up.

Deploy might be one of the unit's METL tasks. The commander assesses how well his unit can deploy and then builds a training plan to improve the unit's ability in that area. One thing's for sure: if the unit doesn't practice the task, its skills will erode—and you don't want to be fumbling around with basics as you're heading off to battle.

As the commander works with the METL he realizes that it's built on individual soldier skills. To stay with the deploy example, the soldier's got to be able to drive the truck, tank, or personnel carrier in a convoy. He's got to be able to drive at night, in a chemical environment, with a gas mask on. The soldier must know how to pull maintenance on the vehicle and shoot straight under attack. These are individual skills that the soldier *must* have.

You've done it right a thousand times in game-type conditions.

There are some things the unit wants to be highly practiced in. These things are called battle drills. They're the things the unit wants to be able to do intuitively, things they can do in their sleep because they do them so well.

An Army unit in convoy, for instance, might have "respond to ambush" as a battle drill. What are the lead vehicles supposed to do? What do they do if the road's blocked? If they have killed or wounded? These are the situations the unit will practice until they know exactly how to respond. They want to get so good that they *hope* the bad guys will try and ambush them. That's the attitude of the battle drill.

The commander will take a building block approach to training. Individual skills come first. Then come small-unit tactics—team, squad, and platoon. When the companies and battalions have their acts together, they can train as brigades and then up to division and beyond.

Think of a field-goal unit in football. The kicker's got to be able to kick, the holder hold, and the center snap the ball accurately and then block. To some degree they can practice these things on their own or among the three of them. But eventually the rest of the unit has got to practice with them. Then they run the battle drill of getting onto the field in 20 seconds, blocking out the other team, and snapping, placing, and kicking the ball. That's something every football team has got to be able to do to be successful, and if the coach doesn't pay attention to this mission essential task, the team's skills will erode.

You never want to go to war with a "see what happens" attitude. The whole point of a good training plan is to be able to demonstrate complete competency when the chips are down. It's the same thing in sports. You don't want to send your field-goal unit out on the field with the feeling that "we'll see what happens." You've trained. You've done it right a thousand times in game-type conditions. Now you're going to demonstrate competency and make it happen.

The Coach's Training Strategy

Before anything happens in the Army, the commander develops his training strategy.

Before anything happens on a sports team, the coach develops his training strategy.

In both cases, the leader must convey his unique approach to training—and practice sessions. Everything that does or doesn't happen in practice flows from the strategy. Everyone in the organization needs to understand this strategy. That way they know what they're doing and why they're doing it. OK, I'm going to play coach and provide a sample strategy. Mine would go something like this:

A Sample Strategy

Everything we do, we do for a reason. My goal is to create an environment of constant learning.

I see myself as the guy in charge of building a better mousetrap. I think of the other team as one point better than us. It's my job to find the point, and then another, and another. Players and assistants can help me in this quest. We must all look for points.

Time is a valuable resource; we will not waste it. My practices will be of relatively short duration, but they will be intense. Players will arrive on time. Early arrival is also authorized. Players will be ready to go.

No opponent will be better conditioned than we are. Players must maintain themselves in top physical condition throughout the year. We will work hard to maintain that edge.

Players are ultimately responsible for their own individual skills and conditioning. Assistants will constantly be on the lookout for opportunity training—providing fundamental instruction so that the player does it right. There's a right way and a wrong way to do everything, and we owe it to our players to teach them the right way.

It's my job to make practice fun. I will keep everyone on edge. We will count and record everything, and I will create an environment where players can compete for starting positions. We will make a "game" of things, because I want a team that loves to compete. Expect to be rewarded for outstanding performance and punished for the substandard.

Expect me and my assistants to be twice as animated in practice as we are in games—teaching is where we earn our pay. Expect us to be excited about getting things right. Then expect us to be quietly confident that the team will get the job done when it counts.

Our players must have their fundamentals down pat. Expect me and my assistants to work hard on anybody who doesn't. Expect to learn fast.

I believe in overlearning—knowing a task so well that it can be done under extreme conditions, which is what competition will bring. The complex builds on the simple, and we will do the simple things to perfection.

We will use drills to reinforce fundamentals and team concepts. Players will focus on mastering drills to reinforce excellence. We will allow no sloppiness. Ever.

We will practice situations intensively—especially overtimes and end-of-game scenarios. Our team will work these situations with a view toward mastering our opponents at crunch time. We will sometimes practice under poor conditions to prepare us for battle. We will know what to do—coaches and players. End time is our time.

Occasionally, I will ask everyone to do things at less than 100 percent. I will tell you those times and how hard I want you to go. Sometimes I will lighten things up and we'll have a few laughs. Sometimes we will need to conserve energy or give ourselves a break. I will decide those times.

I want everyone to understand the "why" of what we are doing. I will try to make that clear, because we do everything for a reason. Players deserve to know what we will be doing in practice on any given day; and we will tell them.

We will play teams with greater sophistication and talent—and we will defeat them. My goal is to establish a solid team foundation from which we can outperform our opponents. Don't expect every solution to come from the coaching staff; ultimately, it is the players who must perform and find a way to win. The foundation is laid in practice.

Well, there you have it. One coach's training philosophy. Simple and direct.

The important thing is the coach's *expression* of his philosophy—getting everybody on the same page. Once a player understands the coach's practice strategy, he can fine-tune his personal practice strategy.

The Player's Practice Strategy

Too many players take the narrow view of practice. They see it as something to be endured, and they practice accordingly, which is not very well.

Players need to tune in to the coach's philosophy even if he doesn't articulate it especially well. See practice as a quest for excellence, regardless of how the coach runs practice. Take responsibility for your

---

17 PRACTICE HARD

You have to have a work ethic, a set of habits on which to establish your practice strategy. If you pace yourself in practice, you aren't hustling. Unconsciously, you'll do the same thing in a game. You get what you practice. So practice hustling.

own improvement. Waiting for the perfect coach, or whining about the present one, won't get it done.

You have to have a work ethic, a set of habits that establish your practice philosophy. It's the "get there early, stay there late" mentality. Are you hustling in practice, or are you looking for shortcuts? If you pace yourself in practice, you aren't hustling. Unconsciously, you'll do the same thing in a game. You get what you practice. So practice hustling. Remember also that you are vying for playing time during team practice. Does "you're always trying out" ring a bell?

Practice concentrating. Don't allow yourself to get bored.

Let's face it: you're practicing either getting better or worse. It's as simple as that. If you're practicing doing things the wrong way, you're reinforcing error. When you practice a skill you're building a neurological pathway that you will follow in the future. That's why you don't repeat mistakes. When you learn mistakes, you actually have to backtrack in order to unlearn them. Life is too short for that kind of process. By the time you get it right, you'll be as old as I am.

Make sure you're learning fundamentally sound techniques. Listen to competent instruction. Listen, and do.

Look, nobody likes to be corrected. Nobody. A kid doesn't like it; a pro doesn't like it. It's part of being human. It's uncomfortable. Answering with, "I've always done it this way," is the easy way out. But it doesn't lead to improvement.

Let me tell you a very sad story.

The other night at a Kansas City Royals baseball game, a fan dropped a little pop-up at the upper-deck railing. This was a guy in his twenties, sitting there with his girlfriend, with a baseball glove. The ball hits his glove and falls into the lower stands.

The crowd booed lustily, it was such a pathetic effort. The guy was humiliated; his girlfriend mortified. Three innings later he was still shaking his head. All his life he waits for a major league baseball, and he muffs his chance in front of his girlfriend and thirty thousand spectators.

But you know what?

He one-handed it. The chance of a lifetime, and he one-hands it. The first thing every kid hears when he walks on a baseball field is: "Two hands!"

Let me tell you something: I've got good hands, and I've caught a million baseballs, but if I'm sitting there with my glove, I'm using two hands. You know how I know that? Because that's how I was trained. That's how I practiced. It's automatic.

You want your fundamentals to be automatic. You want to establish good work habits and good fundamental habits. It takes the pressure off. You won't be having an internal debate when a major league baseball is staring you in the face.

Once you get the fundamentals down, you can tinker with the fine points. That's what good players do. As they're practicing, they're tinkering, looking for the little things that will fine-tune their game.

Golfers are the biggest tinkerers. Once the swing is fundamentally sound, a golfer will tinker, fiddle with this and fiddle with that, always looking for something to grab onto to get through a tournament or a round. Sometimes it involves a mental picture, like swinging through the ball; sometimes it's a minor physical adjustment, like softening the grip. The golfer imbeds the adjustment, and when he doesn't need to think about it any longer, he tinkers some more.

Golfers also make major use of ritual—a preset pattern of actions to get ready to hit the ball. The golfer will select a club, look at his lie, pick out his target from behind the ball, stretch, move toward the ball, take a practice swing, set up on the ball, adjust stance, address the ball, adjust to target, and trigger the swing. He does it the same way every time. He doesn't have to reinvent the process for every swing—he relies on habit. He makes it a ritual.

Perfect your own rituals, whether it's free-throw shooting, stepping up to the plate, or setting up for a field goal. Practice provides you the opportunity to do that.

Practice concentrating. Don't allow yourself to get bored.

I've spent a large part of my life as a third baseman. A good 99 percent of my time at third base is spent being ready for the 1 percent of the action that comes my way. The key to success is always

---

18 DON'T REPEAT MISTAKES

Learn the correct fundamentals, and practice performing them correctly. When you learn mistakes, you actually have to backtrack in order to unlearn them. Life is too short for that kind of process.

---

being ready, always expecting the ball. And the key to being ready is to practice being ready, even through baseball practices that would otherwise be boring. It's called "extended concentration."

Playing third base is a lot like life. You practice being ready, you become ready, and when the ball comes your way, you know what to do with it.

Last, do your homework.

Whether it's extra work after practice, studying football plays, or mentally rehearsing what moves you're going to make—you've got to do your homework.

When you've got your individual act together, you're ready to maximize your practice time with the team.

The Art of the Battle Drill

The Soviets had plenty of weakness on their western front, but they had the art of the battle drill down to a science. Their tactics weren't innovative and didn't allow for much creativity; those were the strengths of NATO. But the Soviets were well trained in battle drills. They could execute their basic tactics day after day and night after night without much rest. That made us nervous. Our biggest fear was that they would roll right over us before we had a chance to respond.

It taught us a lot about battle drills.

We discovered that we could take some of the Soviet strengths and adopt them. We did more drilling. We found that in the stress of combat our units could still rely on what they had down to a drill. When the unit was tired and the chance for creativity was low, soldiers could still perform what they had drilled.

The lesson is true in sports. A wrestler will usually forget what he learned that week in practice when he's into a tough match; the stress will cause him to revert to his basics, to what he knows best.

While practice is a time for innovation and adaptation, it's also a time to drill the mission essential tasks, to get them down to a battle drill—one that will stand the test of competition.

TRAIN TOUGH CHALLENGE

- Come to practice with a "make it happen" attitude.

- Practice doing it right. Listen; learn; tinker. Make the fundamentals automatic.

- Ritualize your set-ups and get-readies.

- Do your homework. Just like Mom said.

7

TEAMWORK—
IT REALLY IS WORK

★

The two most important things in life are good friends and a strong bullpen.

—BOB LEMON

Nickie "Little Napoleon" Rojas was my kind of soldier. At four feet, eleven inches she was a tough kid and a legend in her own mind—given to carrying an M-203 grenade launcher wherever she went. She'd been in the Army for only a short time, yet she seemed to know everything about everything—where to get a vehicle fixed, how to get an action through the company bureaucracy, which mess hall was serving steak for dinner.

Nick had a devil-may-care swagger and a military bearing that fired me up every day. In a unit where the stress level was off the chart, her brand of confidence was a constant charge. We fed off each other.

I was a major at the time, and she was a private. At the first opportunity I made her my right hand—she became my driver, personal assistant, and virtual bodyguard. Teaming up with Private Rojas was the first critical step in building my team during a challenging stint in a mechanized infantry unit stationed in Germany at the tail end of the cold war. We were unstoppable.

Nick and I had an understanding. Her job was to kill the close-in bad guys, so I had time to figure out how to kill the ones on the other side of the hill. I could give Nick the tough missions, and she accepted them all with enthusiasm. It wasn't long before she had a chest full of ribbons and a corporal's stripe.

My standard of a teammate has always been whether or not I'd want the person in my foxhole with the enemy in full attack. Whom do I want to be feeding me ammo when it's all on the line? With some soldiers you just know they'll have the machine gun blazing away. With others you're not so sure. Nick was one of the ones I was sure about. She was one of those soldiers you'd have to hold back from attacking into the teeth of an enemy assault.

It was obvious Little Napoleon was headed for bigger things. When she told me she wanted to become an officer, I recommended her for Officer Candidate School. The request was denied; they said she was too short. So we tried again six months later and she was accepted. Maybe she grew a little bit. Most people would have given up the first time. Just like Napoleon Bonaparte, Nick became an officer in the Field Artillery, one of the Army's most demanding career fields. I pity the enemy that comes under fire from a Nickie Rojas barrage. She will bring holy hellfire.

The Army's done a number of studies, all of which confirm the same thing—in combat, soldiers don't fight for Mom, apple pie, or the American way. They fight for one thing—the respect and lives of their buddies. They fight for their team.

Loser Mentality: This team stinks.
Train Tough Attitude: This team can rock the world.

It's a Chemistry Lab

High school chemistry teaches that there's a formula for everything. You can represent the quality and quantity of just about anything with a piece of chalk and a blackboard. Some stuff mixes together just fine, and some stuff doesn't. There's nothing terribly mysterious about chemistry, once you grasp the basics. With the right mix of chemicals—under the right conditions—you can manufacture some powerful stuff. It's the same way in sports.

Some teams just seem to have the right chemistry. The players fit together like molecules, and the result is always more than the sum of the parts. Other teams are characterized by a seemingly unending series of explosions, or worse, a puddle of gunk where nothing happens.

So the question becomes, how do you manufacture a functioning team?

Well, the first thing you've got to have is the right stuff. No big secret here. You've got to have some real players—the ones who are going to carry the ball and compete. These are the players who are going to be candidates for the all-conference or all-star team. If you're lucky, these guys are leaders; you're going to need some leadership from somewhere, and it's best if it comes from the most talented players.

Then you've got to have role players, those who are willing to bunt, hit-and-run, rebound, or punt. Guys who are willing to do the dirty work that winning requires. And you need some people who can come off the bench with egos intact, ready to get a job done.

> *You want your big guns performing with the game on the line, and it takes a team to get them there.*

Every team needs a clown, somebody to occasionally point out the absurdity of it all. There's always going to be bad juju for any team to deal with; it helps to be able to laugh about it.

What you don't need are the misfits, the ones who have the potential to produce but who consistently find ways to come up short. These are the 10 percent who cause 90 percent of the problems. These people deserve a chance, but when the chance is over, they need to go somewhere else. Michael Jordan used to drive these kinds of guys off his team. He made their lives so miserable they either quit outright or asked to be traded.

Sometimes the best thing for a misfit is to go somewhere else where he might fit in. But usually the problem is bigger than that. The Navy calls it ballast, but by whatever name, dead weight is dead weight. Those who don't contribute need to be contributed somewhere else.

Building a team takes commitment. There must be concrete expectations and standards. Egos must be kept in check. Conflicts must be resolved. But remember, this is a sports team we're building here, not a sewing group.

Team cohesion is built around a task; social cohesion outside the task is secondary. Most of the bonding takes place on the field or in the gym. Singing all 26 verses of *Kumbaya* is not going to make it. This is especially true for men. Men bond around the task; women respond more to the personal connection, where relationships are sometimes as important as the game itself.

As a teammate I could care less about your police record as long as you can deliver the ball. What you do on your own time is of little interest to me; I care only about what you're doing on our time. That person in the stands could be your preacher or your parole officer; it really doesn't matter as long as you're taking care of business.

Somebody once said, "There is no *I* in *team*," but that's true on only a superficial level; after all, there is an *I* in *win*. Team players should still have individual goals, as long as they're subordinate to the goals of the team—that is, winning. You want your big guns performing with the game on the line, and it takes a team to get them there.

Witness the 1998 NBA championship–winning final shot of Michael Jordan's stupendous career with the Chicago Bulls. Remember that Scottie Pippen played that game in excruciating back pain. Remember too the misfits that weren't there to get in the way—Jordan himself having made sure those guys were long gone.

It's easy to recall Jordan's great move on Utah's Bryon Russell and the beauty of his final shot. What's less memorable is what his teammates were doing at the same time to help make the shot happen—Tony Kukoc and Steve Kerr positioning themselves as scoring threats and Dennis Rodman cutting from the high post to position himself for the possibility of a rebound.

Whether Scottie and Michael watched cartoons together on Saturday mornings wasn't a factor in their on-court friendship. Who partied with Dennis Rodman was irrelevant.

The '90s Bulls always had more than their share of internal strife, but they had a winning chemistry on the floor.

Winning hides a multitude of sins. The stress of losing compounds any interpersonal problems a team is having. That's why winning is always the ultimate team builder and why there really is no substitute for victory.

In sports, as in war, the winners write the history books.

My Black Brothers

I grew up in a lily-white environment. My school district was 99.9 percent white, and there were probably a lot more nines behind that decimal than I have space to include. I think there was one black kid in a neighboring school, otherwise that lily would have been a complete albino.

The race riots of the late '60s scared the heck out of me. Malcolm X also made an impression. It wasn't until I went to prep school my last two years of high school that I mixed it up with some black students and found out how much fun the whole experience could be. It was like foreign travel for me. Our basketball team sponsored numerous clinics in inner-city neighborhoods, and I stayed in several neighborhood homes. Despite the racial tensions of the times, everybody I met went out of their way to make me feel comfortable. My experience with black people got off to a very good start.

That uniform is a powerful thing; so is the team-building process of working together for a common goal.

The Army of the '70s was a racial melting pot. To the Army's credit, it made a frontal assault on racial prejudice, and despite some tough battles, it was a war that was an overall win. We had "rap sessions" where soldiers got together with a trained leader and talked out the various issues of the day. For the first time, I got to walk a mile or two in the other guy's combat boots. I could see where that could be a pretty tough mile.

About that time I read *The Autobiography of Malcolm X*—an important work that I've read a couple times since. Brother Malcolm's journey, though challenging in the extreme, is not unlike the journey many Americans, myself included, have had to take in understanding the race challenge in the United States. As bad as the situation has been in our past, and despite the problems that continue to this day, we're fortunate to be in a place where we have a good chance to move forward—to finally live up to our ideals.

Putting on a uniform, whether that of a soldier or an athlete, is the best thing that ever happened to race relations. A uniform is a symbol of team, a symbol that team colors are more important than skin colors. Even the borderline bigot will find himself cheering for the black athlete when that player is carrying the ball for his favorite team. We just need to find a way to translate that enthusiasm and tolerance into everyday life. Maybe it would help if we could see that as Americans we're already on the same team.

Try this on for size. I figure I've played on nearly one hundred different teams in my career. Some of those teams were all white, and some of the teams we played against were all black. It's my observation that the most effective sports teams are the ones with a mix. It's almost as if the glue that bonds the mix becomes stronger than the ingredients in the mix. That uniform is a powerful thing; so is the team-building process of working together for a common goal. The team is a great place to feel the melding together of players of different backgrounds and ethnicity—whether you're in the Army or on the playing field.

Communicating the Team Message

In communication, little things mean a lot. In fact, it's the little things that communicate the most.

Words are cheap, and actions speak louder than words. In the Army we sometimes communicate by way of briefings. "Brief me," the general will say. That means start with the bottom line and be ready to shut up. "Be brief, be brilliant, be gone," is a motto that has saved many military careers—including mine. I was a natural big-mouth who learned to keep his big mouth shut—until I had something important to contribute.

Good team players know when to keep their mouth shut—which is most of the time. When you do need to speak, your words will carry a lot more weight if you haven't already made an ass of yourself popping off and being stupid.

The most important way to communicate with your teammates is to honor the team standards by exceeding them. That means showing up early and staying late. That means running your wind sprints past the finish line. In everything you do, you project a professional image and work ethic. You do your job.

Do your job. That's what your teammates expect. You can be the nicest person in the world, but if you're stumbling and fumbling, you can't be on my team. Your ability to do your job is what the team depends on.

Communication with your teammates should be positive and complimentary. Go out of your way to say hi, and smile when you say it. These are the people who are going to make your day. You ought to be happy to see them.

> *Do your job. That's what your teammates expect. You can be the nicest guy in the world, but if you're stumbling and fumbling, you can't be on my team.*

As a coach I'm not afraid to dog out a player, but as a teammate I almost never do. I focus on keeping my body language positive even after a teammate boots the big one. Like I say, little things mean a lot.

As a third baseman I learned that it's counterproductive to exhort the pitcher to throw strikes—he's already trying to do that. You get much better results by simply praising every pitch. "Good shot, Mike," is a lot better than "C'mon, Mike."

It's the same way with hitters. The best thing you can do for a hitter with runners on base is to praise the player who just got on base. That way the batter knows if he comes through he'll be praised too. That's a lot better than begging the poor guy to "get a hit."

---

19 COMMUNICATE

The most important way of communicating with your teammates is to honor the team standards by exceeding them. That means showing up early and staying late. That means running your wind sprints past the finish line. In everything you do, you project a professional image and work ethic. Communication with your teammates should be positive and complimentary. Go out of your way to say hi, and smile when you say it. These are the people who are going to make your day. You ought to be happy to see them. Then do your job. That's what your team-mates expect.

Since developing a jump shot in basketball, I've become so sensitive to subtleties that I can tell if a teammate has confidence in my shot by the way he passes me the ball. I've become a better passer as a result. When I dish a teammate the ball I send a big "go get 'em"— I try to convey the feeling that it's all his basketball and I believe he can knock it down.

Little things mean a lot.

A Word About Weirdos

I've played on so many teams that I sometimes see players as replaceable cogs in a machine. Most of my teammates are in the past now; many are largely forgotten, with even the unforgettable a bit of a blur.

I don't need to know your name for you to be on my team. I only want to know what you bring to the banquet—a baron of beef or a ham sandwich. Maybe that's cold, but I need to know if what you've got will match my contribution.

It's probably good that everybody's different, that it takes all kinds to make a team.

Some guys are weird. They're different. They come at the thing from a whole different perspective. You've got to make room for them too.

One guy I know seemed like a pretty good ballplayer, but he kept screwing up on the field. Something was wrong with this guy. Then one Saturday we played a tournament. The guy went out and packed his ice chests with drinks for everybody. In between games we'd collapse around his truck and suck up his beverages. And the guy played great all day. Now this was an act of brotherhood that would never have occurred to me. Not in a thousand years. But you know what? That's what it took for this guy to feel part of the team. He needed to feel some connection beyond the battleground.

And, hey, I'm OK with that. I have no problem with free drinks. Who knows, maybe I'm the weirdo.

Like a Freight Train, Baby

I spent a good part of my life getting ready to fight the Soviets. Now that was a mixed-up crew, so it's only appropriate they wound up in last place and lost their franchise.

One of the few things they talked about that made any sense was that bit about the "collective will of the people." They never really had it—which is a good thing—but they bragged about it a lot.

Collective will is a freight train roaring down the tracks at a hundred miles an hour. Better get out of the way. It's unstoppable. When a team has players with willpower, that willpower can become collective will. When that happens, Baby, watch out.

How does a team of willpower players take on collective will? By clearly articulating high expectations. By somebody stating what the goals are and having the whole team commit to them.

That's it. That's what it takes.

Now get to practice.

20 GET ON BOARD

Collective will is like a freight train roaring down the track at a hundred miles an hour. Better get out of the way. When a team has players with willpower, that willpower can become collective will. It's unstoppable.

TRAIN TOUGH CHALLENGE

- Think of yourself as a catalyst, a chemical term for the substance that makes things happen.

- Do your job. Do it well. Make that *real* well.

- Wear the uniform with pride; it's the outward symbol of the team.

- Get positive. Stay positive. And pass it on.

- Buy into the team goals, and hop aboard the freight train.

8

THE M. C. BENDER LEADERSHIP ACADEMY

★

A good military leader must dominate the events which encompass him; once events get the better of him he will lose the confidence of his men, and when that happens he ceases to be of value as a leader.
— FIELD MARSHAL BERNARD MONTGOMERY

The M. C. Bender Leadership Academy has always been a bit of a cruel joke in the Bender family.

The academy was founded for the wayward Bender children whenever summer vacation became too much for them to handle. Failing to accomplish chores, bickering with Mom or each other, and taking on a bored, "thousand-yard" stare made one a candidate for the academy. The academy was named for its founder, commandant, and guiding light—me.

Enrollment was swift and uncompromising.

"Congratulations," I would begin, in drill sergeant voice, "you are now enrolled in the M. C. Bender Leadership Academy. The academy will introduce you to a new way of life. Goals will be set and accomplished. We will teach you to read great books, work and play hard, and excel across a broad range of endeavors. You will attain a high state of physical fitness, while maintaining esprit de corps and a can-do attitude. Those who cannot meet the standards will be recycled. Graduation is scheduled for one week from today. Now drop down and give me 50 push-ups—*and I do not mean Air Force push-ups!*"

Cadets began a rigorous curriculum of planned activities that molded them into lean, mean little fighting machines. They were allowed only one communication with the outside world—"I'm in the academy this week." Their pals found this to be synonymous with "the Bender kids are away at camp."

Graduation day was as much anticipated as the dreaded threat of "recycle" was feared. No one wanted to do extra time at the academy. Graduation was cause for celebration.

I'm proud to say that all four of our children are now graduates of the academy. Though it's still a little early to tell what, if any, effect the experience has had on their lives, the early indications are positive. We hope to have all the kids back for Founder's Day.

Average Joe: I'll stay out of the way. No one will notice me.
Train Tough Attitude: I'll go first. Follow me.

Everyone's a Leader

The Leadership Academy was a take-off from my Army experience, where we preach that everyone's a leader, no matter how far down the totem pole they function. The lowliest privates are leaders. If they do their job and do it well, they have a positive influence on those around them—they're leaders. But you've got to be able to follow before you lead. You've got to have control of yourself.

Nickie "Little Napoleon" Rojas, even as a private, was my emotional leader. She set the pace every day—upbeat, energetic, fearless. While as a major I was calling the shots, Little Napoleon was providing the spark. She set the tone for the team.

The U.S. military believes that leadership can be learned. From the first moments of a recruit's life, we teach leadership. First, we set the example. Everything we do says "be like me." We want the soldiers to see leaders that they can look up to, that they can emulate.

Then we place the soldiers in leadership positions and critique their performance in accordance with our leadership doctrine. Some are natural leaders and some struggle. But everybody gets a chance, and we find that most—sooner or later—get the hang of it. The soldiers' promotions indicate their readiness for increased leadership responsibilities, and they find themselves in charge of more soldiers and larger units. The leadership training never stops; at every career juncture we're pitching a style of leadership commensurate with the leader's level of responsibility.

> *You don't have to join the Army to get the leadership bug.*

You don't have to join the Army to get the leadership bug. Sports provide every bit as good a venue to develop your leadership style.

Think of yourself as a leader. Conduct yourself so as to have a positive influence on your teammates.

Even if you're the new kid on the block, you demonstrate leadership by the way you conduct yourself. Quiet at first, you slowly but powerfully exert the force of your personality on others. You accomplish this by doing—by demonstrating that you have control of yourself and are fit to lead others. Leadership is a trust that is earned.

The Three Cs of Team Leadership

Regardless of your particular role on a team, you're a leader. Everyone's a leader. You're leading in either a positive manner or a negative manner. You're either a positive or negative influence. The Three Cs of Leadership will keep you positive.

---

21 LEAD THE WAY

Think of yourself as a leader. Demonstrate leadership by the way you conduct yourself. Quiet at first, and deferential, you slowly but powerfully exert the force of your personality on others. You accomplish this by doing—by demonstrating that you have control of yourself and are fit to lead others. Leadership is a trust that is earned.

Competence

OK, competence is not a very sexy concept, but it's the foundation of leadership. You've got to know your stuff. You must be able to execute the fundamentals and perform them on the playing field.

Are you positioned at the front of every teaching session? Or are you cowering in the back? Are you the first through every drill or waiting for someone else to show the way? Are you doing your homework or just getting by?

If you're like most players, you can't give a positive response to all of these questions. But it's not too late. Challenge yourself to deepen your understanding of your sport and master the fundamentals. Be the first in line to try a new technique. Lead the way.

Courage

Leaders become leaders through an instinctual process. There's the instinct of the leader to assert himself and the instinct of the group to choose its leaders. Courage is the most important criteria. Human beings look for leaders to demonstrate courage, to lead from the front. It comes in two parts: physical courage and character.

Physical courage occurs on the playing field. It's a willingness to take risks, to commit to a work ethic, and, most of all, to sacrifice. It's Jason Kidd playing with three screws in his ankle in the 2000 NBA playoffs and again with stitches above his eye in 2002 . . . playing in pain, when he knew he couldn't be at his best, but when he knew his team had to have him to have a chance.

Character is the other half of the equation. Leaders must be trusted to do the right thing when it counts. While they may not be angels, we must trust them in the things that matter. We expect them to make the right choice between team success and personal glory. Off the field, character is a plus; on the field it's a must.

Competitiveness

Competitiveness is catching. It starts with leaders and infects the whole team. Conversely, when leaders retreat in the face of challenge, the rest of the team follows.

Leaders challenge teammates to compete. They communicate the message by what they say and what they do. Competitiveness takes audacity—an audacity applied to the quest of winning, the animal desire to get it on with a worthy opponent, to match the attack blow for blow. It's using your opponent to drive you to ever-increasing heights of performance. It's not for the faint of heart.

Leaders have it in spades.

Communication—the Fourth C of Team Leadership

I joined the military at the end of the Vietnam War. At the time, the nation's military and political leaders had turned denial and avoidance into art forms. Communication was poor; morale was low. Drug use was rampant. The term "credibility gap" accurately described the difference between what was said and the reality of a given situation.

With the end of the war came a tremendous housecleaning. Secretary of the Army Bo Callaway started a "Glad You Asked" campaign. We thought it was a joke at first, but it actually worked. Instead of leaders avoiding questions and skirting issues, they started telling the truth, even when it hurt. It was as if a great wind swept through the Army and blew away the ashes of the Vietnam mentality.

We learned the benefits of honest communication.

When we fought the Gulf War 15 years later, the same TV cameras appeared with the same questions reporters had asked during Vietnam. Only this time our soldiers knew how to respond, because

---

⭐ 22 BE A COMPETITOR

Leaders challenge teammates to compete. They communicate the message verbally and nonverbally, by what they say and what they do. Competitiveness takes audacity. Competitiveness is audacity applied to the quest of winning, the animal desire to get it on with a worthy opponent, to match the attack blow for blow. It's using your opponent to drive you to ever-increasing heights of performance. It is not for the faint of heart. Leaders have competitiveness in spades.

every soldier knew the objective was to kick Saddam Hussein out of Kuwait. It was a simple, stated objective that was effectively communicated to every soldier. We had everybody on the same page— and it paid huge dividends.

Frankly, communication is the biggest challenge leaders face in the sports arena. Our tendency as athletes is to close up and deal with problems internally. We don't like tough questions. Our communication is often coded and brief, like a play called in a football huddle. It's efficient but not necessarily effective.

> *The leader must keep his game face.*

Leaders need to put themselves in their teammates' cleats once in a while and get the other perspective. Leaders need to listen. A player riding the bench wants to know why he's there and wants to understand what his role is. A leader will listen and instruct.

Everything communicates. Leaders who say the goal is a championship but party the night before a game won't have much credibility.

Leaders who communicate the vision of a championship do so creatively and emphatically. They vary the message so it will be accepted and absorbed. They communicate verbally and nonverbally, knowing that actions speak even louder than words. Strong leaders find creative ways to inspire teammates, and they always set the example.

When Leaders Fail

I was privileged to serve with British forces for three years. We are fortunate to have them as allies. They are extremely well disciplined, well trained, and, most important, unflappable.

They have a saying that pretty well sums up their attitude toward life: "The king is dead; long live the king." The death of the leader is a statement of fact; the consolation is simply that there's another to follow behind. May he have long life.

Leaders fall, and leaders fail. They strike out, fumble, and drop the ball. There's always a bit of extra trauma when leaders fail. But when you're a leader, you can't let it get to you. You can't quit, not even for a minute.

Players will accept the leader's failing; after all, they accept that leaders are human. But they will not respect leaders who quit.

The leader must keep his game face. He must demonstrate resiliency, both mentally and physically. Mentally, he must immediately show that his spirit has not been broken. Physically, he must demonstrate his continued commitment to perform.

Leaders play through the tough moments, gathering energy from the challenge. Their teammates will follow.

The Thin Red Line

The Thin Red Line was a disturbing movie. I saw it a week after I got out of the Army, and it reminded me how lucky I was to have spent 24 years in the business without a visit to hell. The film deals with an important question: "What does it take to get men to take the hill?" The answer, though murky, is leadership.

Nick Nolte plays the colonel. Early on we see him brownnosing with a general who insinuates that the colonel's future promotions

---

23 PICK YOURSELF UP

Leaders fall, and leaders fail. They strike out, fumble, and drop the ball. There's always a bit of extra trauma when leaders fail. But when you're a leader, you can't let it get to you. You can't quit, not even for a minute. Players will accept the leader's failing; after all, they accept that leaders are human. But they will not respect leaders who quit. The leader must keep his game face. He must demonstrate mental and physical resiliency. Mentally, he must immediately show that his spirit has not been broken. Physically, he must demonstrate his continued commitment to perform. Leaders play through the tough moments, gathering energy from the challenge. Their teammates will follow.

will hinge on how the next operation goes. It's World War II. The next operation will be the bloodbath of Guadalcanal.

It's clear that the colonel wants his promotion. It's also clear that the operation is an important one—the fight for the island's airfield will determine whether the Japanese or the Americans will control the skies, and ultimately the South Pacific.

What really drives the colonel? Promotion? Mission? Or both? Whatever it is, the colonel becomes a madman, fanatically driven to see the mission accomplished—regardless of the human cost.

Caught in the middle is Captain Starles, a good man who has spent two years with his men and has come to value their lives. Starles is a sympathetic character—we see him praying for courage and attending to the needs of his soldiers.

> *The colonel had what it took to transform tired, terrified men into a team.*

The mission quickly goes south. Captain Starles watches as his men die in what seems a senseless slaughter. The colonel's on the radio screaming for him to keep pushing. Starles reports that the enemy is dug in and has too much firepower—he wants to try a flanking movement. The colonel denies his request and orders a frontal assault. Starles, seeing the order as certain suicide for his men, refuses to move. The colonel, in a rage, orders him to hold on until he gets there.

The colonel takes charge. He seems crazy—cajoling the men, ranting and raving. He stands while they cower. They are scared, terrorized at the deaths of their comrades and paralyzed by the prospect of more fighting. When a mortar round explodes nearby, the colonel doesn't flinch. His presence breathes new life into the men. He explains the situation and asks for volunteers. He gets his volunteers, and the men take the hill. That mission accomplished, he continues driving the men forward, sensing that further gains can be made while the enemy is beating a hasty retreat.

At the next opportunity, the colonel fires Captain Starles. To avoid a flap, he offers Starles a stateside assignment and medals he does not deserve. Starles takes him up on it. Later, Starles's replacement will panic under pressure.

There's nothing very uplifting about *The Thin Red Line*. It offers a realistic view of the horrors of war, with all its chaos, immorality, and senselessness. But it's an important film because of what it shows us about leadership.

The leader, in this case a colonel, has imperfect motivation. He functions from a mix of self-promotion and the desire to see an important mission through. He's not very likable. He's not very smart. He seems crazy. He's an uncaring jerk. But he has the courage to move forward into the battle zone. He shares the hazards of battle with his men, and he stands as an example of fearlessness. He communicates his vision of the battle and demonstrates competence in devising a plan. His competitive fire never wavers.

The colonel has what it takes to transform tired, terrified men into a team. He is able to get into the minds of a group of soldiers who had decided their mission was hopeless. He has what it takes to drive them up that hill—the ability to lead, ugly though it was.

Becoming a Better Leader

Because I believe everyone's a leader, we'll begin with the assumption that you're already a leader and that you're a positive force. Naturally, you want to become a better leader and take on more of a leadership role.

The best way to learn leadership is to coach.

Those Three Cs—competence, courage, competitiveness—take on a whole new meaning when you're looking for them from the helm. Coaching opens up a whole new vista on leadership.

The level of coaching doesn't matter—you can learn a lot by coaching kids. Kids will both exhilarate and exasperate. Sometimes they'll catch the spirit in ways that will amaze you, and sometimes they'll shock you with the realization that their little minds can be so closed at such an early age. It's almost like they're human.

You'll see what happens when your star player had "a sleepover at Damian's" the night before a game . . . what it's like when your best players have a bad day. You'll learn how to restrain yourself from trying to shake some sense into all of them.

You begin to see what happens when players are focused and what happens when they're not. You'll see a little of yourself in each kid. But be prepared—it might not be pretty.

The best way to learn is to teach. Fundamentals take on a whole new relevance when you're coaching them. You'll find ways to keep the "fun" in fundamentals. And you'll see that fundamentals pay off. One of my greatest moments on the planet was seeing a young player of mine box out the other team's big guy in the final seconds of a championship basketball tournament. He did what we taught him. Way to go, Michael Pearson!

When things click, you're a genius. Putting Johnny in to pinch run was pure brilliance. The boys caught fire under your dynamic leadership. The team came a long way.

Through it all you learn responsibility, something you can fully appreciate only by being in charge. The mundane matters of equipment, scheduling, and lineup cards will all be yours. Your perspective as a player will never be the same.

So get out there, Coach.

TRAIN TOUGH CHALLENGE

- Enroll in the Leadership Academy. Plan on getting control of yourself before you lead others.

- Make yourself a student of leadership. Master the Three Cs—competence, courage, and competitiveness.

- Understand that as a leader you will sometimes fall. Get very good at getting back up.

- Get a coaching position. Ask yourself: "What's wrong with those kids?" Then look within. Good luck, Coach.

PART THREE

LET THE BATTLE BEGIN
THIS IS WHAT WE LIVE FOR, THIS IS HOW WE DO IT

9

KNOW YOUR ENEMY

★

If one does not plan and takes the enemy lightly, one will certainly be captured by him.

—SUN TZU, THE ART OF WAR, 300 B.C.

Using the word *enemy* to describe a sports opponent might be a bit strong. That's why I like it.

Err on the side of the dramatic when thinking about your opponent. Get the creative juices flowing. Find a way to beat the guy.

Even though the other guys are only a simulated enemy, it helps to think of them as the enemy. It's part of the game. Nobody's going to get hurt or break the rules. We're still going to be good sports—but we're also going to let off some good, healthy steam.

"Know your enemy" is a military adage. The idea is to know your enemy's tactics, weaponry, and thinking so that you can take advantage of him. You want to get inside his head and learn how he reacts, makes decisions, and operates. That way you can protect yourself, deceive him about your true intentions, and create surprise by doing something he doesn't expect.

Typical Jock Mentality: I'll just worry about my own game.

Train Tough Attitude: How can I get inside this guy's head and fake him out?

It's in the Bible

The concept of deception puts us in a moral gray area. There's no doubt that deceit is a major problem in human relationships and that the search for truth occupies the thinking of most of the world's religions. Still, deception seems to be OK if it's practiced with reasonable cause. The Bible has numerous instances where the good guys faked out their pursuers.

Rahab hid the Israelite spies in stalks of flax. When the Jericho police came by, she told them, "They went thataway." Then she let the spies down the city walls on a rope and told them to hide out in the hills for a while.

When the apostle Paul was threatened in Damascus, his pals waited until nightfall and lowered him out of town through a hole in the wall—while he hid in a basket. Should he have walked out the front gate? I don't think so.

Just as sure as the world is full of tough calls, sports are full of head fakes, ball fakes, and curveballs. The whole idea is to keep your opponent off balance. Maybe it's all just practice for when we have to use the same tactics against our real enemies.

Military Applications

Sun Tzu

Ancient Chinese history is chock-full of fake-outs. They had the art of deception down to a science. The Chinese philosopher-general Sun Tzu wrote about these strategies some 2,500 years ago in *The Art of War*.

"If you know the enemy and know yourself," he wrote, "you need not fear the result of a hundred battles."

Sun Tzu had a right to talk—his armies were consistently victorious over their enemies. "What enables the general to strike, conquer, and achieve things beyond the reach of ordinary men, is foreknowledge," he concluded.

The Chinese were always pulling stunts on each other. "Force the enemy into a state of confusion—and then crush him," exhorted Sun Tzu.

One commander during that era had his lead troops commit suicide as they met the enemy in battle. The attackers were shocked and distracted, at which time the commander counterattacked to take advantage of the confusion. His suicidal soldiers were men that had already been condemned to death, who chose instead to die by their own hand.

Spartacus

If there were a Gladiator Hall of Fame, Spartacus would head the list of inductees. Hailing from the independent country of Thrace, Spartacus was drafted against his will into the Roman Army, from which he escaped. Recaptured by the Romans, he was sold into slavery and became a gladiator at the Capuan School, known for centuries as the "Headquarters of Gladiators."

Apparently, Spartacus learned his lessons well. He organized a breakout with 70 fellow gladiators, armed with kitchen utensils. Incredibly, the men not only fought off the school staff but escaped the city, driving back pursuers as they went and acquiring actual weapons from their victims.

Spartacus and his men hid out on Mount Vesuvius, from which they raised a rebel army of slaves from the countryside. They would repeatedly outwit the Roman legions who came to do battle. When enveloped by the troops of the proconsul Publius Varinius, Spartacus had his men place stakes at short intervals around the camp. They then set up corpses, dressed in clothes and furnished with weapons, to give the appearance of sentries. He also lit fires throughout the camp. Deceiving the enemy by this empty show, Spartacus and his men quietly slipped away that night.

Spartacus would defeat two Roman armies and conquer most of southern Italy before Rome could subdue him.

Paul Revere

The other side of surprise is security; that is, protecting your own force and ensuring you don't get surprised. There is no better lesson in security than the midnight ride of Paul Revere.

In 1775, General Thomas Gage, the British commander-in-chief of the Massachusetts Bay Colony, was instructed to enforce order among the colonists. Fat chance.

Gage gave Lieutenant Colonel Francis Smith secret orders to take a detachment of seven hundred British soldiers to Concord to destroy supplies and arrest Samuel Adams and John Hancock. Smith began assembling his men on Boston Common on the evening of April 18. The colonists knew something was up. Paul Revere was sent to warn Adams and Hancock at Lexington and the Patriots at Concord.

Revere began his journey at 10 P.M., crossing Boston Harbor by boat and borrowing a horse on the other side. He covered 13 miles on horseback, knocking on doors and spreading word of the British plan. Soon church bells and drums sounded the alarm throughout the countryside, rousing the minutemen from their sleep. Revere arrived in Lexington a couple hours later, where he personally warned Adams and Hancock of the plot to capture them.

When the British arrived in Lexington at dawn the following day, they were surprised to find the minutemen ready to do battle. Shots were fired. The British then found themselves opposed by more minutemen as they marched on Concord—where they were confronted and beaten.

The battles brought out streams of colonists joining the cause of liberty, and the British withdrew to Boston, where they and their comrades soon found themselves besieged by 15,000 New England militiamen.

Fake-Outs, American Style

Compared to most civilizations, the United States has done pretty well living up to the ideal of telling the truth. But go to war with us, and all bets are off. We're going to try and fake you out.

War is a lot easier when you keep your opponent off balance. That's why in every operation we have what's called the "deception plan." It's nothing more than figuring out what we'd like the enemy to think and then doing a bunch of things that will cause him to think that way. In a lot of cases that simply means helping him think what he already wants to think. We just reinforce his misconceptions of how the war will be fought—then we do something entirely different.

At every phase of an operation we're asking, "Does what we're doing support the deception plan? Or is it giving us away?"

Take a look at these great-American fake-outs:

D Day

How do you hide the largest amphibious invasion in the history of the world?

Well, first, you get inside the enemy's decision cycle, which the allies did early in the war. With our breaking of the German communication system and code, we had what's been called the "Ultra Secret"—the communications among Hitler and his generals. We always knew what they were doing and thinking. It was like being inside their huddle on every play. Through constant vigilance and security, we were able to keep this our little secret throughout the war. Nobody knew who didn't need to know. Even Vice President Harry Truman didn't know—until he became president.

We knew Hitler expected the invasion to come at Calais; Calais was the shortest distance across the English Channel and the most direct route to Paris and beyond. So we reinforced Hitler's misconception. We made sure the area saw more than its share of preparatory bombing.

Then we started parachuting mannequins. The Germans soon tired of chasing them around.

When the real soldiers parachuted in, the Germans had let their guard down. Field Marshal Erwin Rommel, in charge of the German defense, was back in Germany on D day. His intelligence crew convinced him it would be a nice, quiet time to go. Besides, it was his wife's birthday. With Rommel out of town, the Germans had a harder time figuring out how to respond. Happy birthday, Helga.

As for Hitler, it took him six weeks to believe the Normandy attack was the real thing. He was fixated on the whereabouts of General George S. Patton, still back in England with a phantom landing force!

Inchon

Although the Korean War was not our finest hour, you have to give General Douglas MacArthur credit for faking out the North Koreans.

With American forces hanging on by a shoestring, MacArthur declared he would land an amphibious force at Inchon—an area known to have extreme tides, making an invasion there most difficult. The North Koreans reasoned that if the Americans were planning a landing at Inchon, the last thing they would do would be announce it.

They figured wrong.

The Inchon landing was a big surprise, effectively cutting the North Korean Army in half.

Desert Storm

Iraq had a land force of 900,000 men, with nearly 6,000 tanks. They were battle hardened from an eight-year war with Iran, in which they had not hesitated to use chemical weapons. Among their weaknesses was a centralized command-and-control system developed in facing the mostly frontal attacks they encountered fighting Iran. Their rigid command-and-control mentality was also a product of Saddam Hussein's dictatorial personality. As long as he could tell them what to do, they would be tough. If we could break down their communication systems, they might have problems reacting.

This we accomplished with air power. We destroyed every means of effective communication the Iraqis had. Soon they were operating blind.

This set up the famous "left hook," where the U.S. VII Corps moved in a wide arc to the west, around Saddam's forces, which were concentrated along the Gulf coast to the east.

A large contingent of Marines were offshore, making it appear as if they were preparing to launch a major amphibious landing—à la Normandy or Inchon. This kept Saddam focused right where we wanted him.

Because this attack never came.

Instead, VII Corps attacked through Iraq to hit the Republican Guard. The extensive Iraqi defenses were useless. Soon hundreds of thousands of Iraqi troops were abandoning dug-in positions only to be picked off by superior U.S. planes, tanks, and artillery.

Saddam never got intelligence on our massive movement to the west, and indeed, he could not have fathomed our ability to move that many men and their equipment so far, so fast. Soon he was fighting our war—on our terms. It was over quickly.

What Does Any of This Have to Do with Sports?

All of this has *everything* to do with sports. Even though the "rules of engagement" are different, the principles are the same. Sports and

---

24 KNOW YOUR ENEMY

The idea is to know your enemy's tactics, weaponry, and thinking so that you can take advantage of him. You want to get inside his head and learn how he reacts, makes decisions, and operates. That way you can protect yourself, deceive him about your true intentions, and create surprise by doing something he doesn't expect. Remember, the whole point of knowing your enemy is so you can run your game on him. Never lose focus on what you have to do. You want to make your enemy play your game.

battle have a lot in common. No, we're not going to bug our opponents' locker room. In fact, we're not going to do anything unethical
or immoral. But we are going to do some things to keep our opponents off balance. The military principles hold true on the sports field.

Know Your Enemy

Learn your enemy's strengths and weaknesses. Find his tendencies.
Know what he likes to do so you can be there before he does it.

If you're playing at a level where you can watch your opponent give
stuff away on TV, then watch him on TV. Watch him on film. Read
about him in the newspaper. If he says something inflammatory, tack
it up on the team bulletin board. Use him for motivation.

Never, ever, underestimate an opponent.

The worst whipping I ever took on a basketball court was from a
little skinny kid, about five feet tall, from Poly Prep. When I matched
up to guard this kid at the start of the game, I saw 35 points in my
future.

I never scored.

But he sure did. This kid beat me every which way until they took
me out. My high school career was never the same. I learned early to
respect the other guy's game.

By the same token, don't make them 10 feet tall.

My brother Tom and I played a lot of ball together. Whenever I'd
get carried away with how great the other guys looked, he'd ask,

---

25 NEVER, *EVER* UNDERESTIMATE AN OPPONENT

There's no such thing as an easy one. All opponents are dangerous.
There are many ways to die on the battlefield and many ways to be surprised on the field of play. Respect your opponent. Respect the fact
that he's trying to defeat you. That makes him dangerous. By the same
token, don't make him 10 feet tall.

"How good can they really be?" That question was always a confidence builder. Sure, they looked good in warm-ups, but we knew from experience that we had what it took to take care of business on the field.

Remember, the whole point of knowing your enemy is so you can run your game on him. Never lose focus on what you have to do. You want to make them play your game.

Secure Your Plan

You've gone to a lot of trouble to build a better mousetrap. Don't give it away.

Remember how the British march on Lexington was discovered? They had poor security.

Remember how the Patriots scrambled to protect their leaders and supplies? They had good security.

Remember who won the war.

I don't even want my opponent to know how I feel about him. Most of the time I'm angry and I want to tear his head off. But I've learned through experience that tearing his head off will be easier if he doesn't know it's coming. So I don't say much. I'm not giving anything away.

"Surprise, Surprise, Surprise"

That's what Gomer Pyle used to say to Sergeant Carter when something really special was about to happen. And we all remember the look on Sergeant Carter's puss. He knew Pyle had him again. You want your opponent to have a Gomer Pyle kind of day—full of surprises. You want him off his rhythm, uncertain and off balance. If you do your job really well, you might even cause him to panic. Hit him with head fakes, ball fakes, and curveballs.

Like a "mark" in a street scam, you want him thinking one way so you can burn him in another.

You can do it within the rules and etiquette of your game.

And you can do it while you're playing *your* game.

TRAIN TOUGH CHALLENGE

- Make a study of your opponent. What do you know about him?

- What's your plan? How will you disguise it?

- What are the ways you can keep your opponent off balance? How can you surprise him?

10

GET READY, GET REALLY READY

★

If I always appear prepared, it is because before entering an undertaking, I have meditated for long and have foreseen what may occur. It is not genius which reveals to me suddenly and secretly what I should do in circumstances unexpected by others; it is thought and meditation.

—NAPOLEON BONAPARTE

The imperial gladiators were often heard praying for the hour of combat.

—EPICTETUS

Let's review where we are.

You're enrolled in the School of the Soldier. Combat U. So far, you're making As.

You've got the combat stance, that matador attitude that creates self-confidence and dominates the bull. You've created a core belief that you deserve to win, that you've done the work. You know your enemy.

You're a supremely conditioned athlete with an always-trying-out attitude. You've made the most of practice time, dedicated yourself to finding a better way, and mastered the fundamentals. You've got it down to a battle drill so that you can perform under the stress of competition. You've toured the M. C. Bender Leadership Academy, where everyone's a leader.

You've got goals. And you've laid the foundation for success. Now it's time to achieve those goals.

It's game day, Baby. And it's going to be a *great* day. Good things are going to happen to you.

Now listen up.

What's coming up in this chapter is going to be the most important stuff in this book. If you could keep only one chapter of *Train Tough the Army Way*, this would be it.

We're going to go step-by-step through a simple process that will absolutely maximize your game-day performance—which is what *Train Tough the Army Way* is all about. All the work leads to game day—all the planning, all the sweat, all the discipline and self-denial. It's time to cash in.

Tired Thinking: I'm really nervous about this one.
Train Tough Attitude: I have seen the future, and it is us.

Let me tell you what's coming.

I'm going to set the table with some general comments about game day and how to plan it. And then I'm going to say some things about attitude. And then we're going to get you in a quiet place where you can get your mind right. And that will be the most important part of this book. Last, we'll take you all the way through warm-ups, right to tip-off, kickoff, or the opening bell.

I *will* have you ready. Brace yourself, and prepare for liftoff.

Reverse Plan Your Game Day

Reverse planning is a military technique designed to ensure there's enough time allotted to accomplish the mission. What we do is establish when we want to take the objective. Then we figure how long the fight will last and how long it will take to get to the battle in the first place. How long do we need to get ready? The answers to all those questions tell us what time we're going to crawl out of our sleeping bags on the day of the battle. We've planned the whole operation in reverse so we're sure there's enough time to get it all accomplished on time.

Do the same thing for game day.

What time does the game start?
When are warm-ups?
How long will it take to dress?
How long is the trip to the arena?
When does the bus leave?
When is the team meal?

When you know the answers to these questions, you not only know what time you're going to get up in the morning, but like a soldier preparing for battle, you have an idea of how your day will go. Sure, there will always be the unexpected events, but you have the basic schedule. Just as reverse planning helps the soldier deal with chaos, it helps the athlete deal with complexity.

What the schedule also tells you is when you will have the time to find a quiet place to get your mind right.

Getting Ready

Yogi Berra said, "Sport is 50 percent physical and 90 percent mental." It's easy to poke fun at Yogi, but in each Yogism there's always a kernel of sheer genius.

Think about it. By game day there's only so much you can do to improve, *physically*. You can't do much to be stronger, faster, or quicker. Beyond rest, the right pregame meal, and a stretch and warm-up, the physical part was determined much earlier. You've set the table for your mind to take over. It's time to reinforce the positive attitudes you've worked so hard to establish and put the final shine on all the hard work you've done.

Game day is here for you to demonstrate competence, to show the world what you can do.

There are three keys to game-day preparation.

Accept Responsibility for Your Mind-Set

You are responsible for how you feel about yourself. Accept this responsibility. Accept it. Just accept it.

Your mind-set does not depend on what other people tell you. They can influence you, but they cannot and must not determine what you think. Only you can do that.

Your past does not determine your mind-set. You can draw on your past for strength and learn from your mistakes, but your past does not determine your mind-set.

Accept responsibility for determining your own mind-set. It's part of your job. It's called mental toughness. It's also called not being intimidated.

Build a Case for Yourself

There's a lot of negativity out there. You must confront your own negative thinking and fears. Some people call it anxiety management. I call it building a case for yourself.

Everybody has negative thoughts. We all have bugaboos.

When Michael Jordan came back to basketball after his baseball experiment, the old Chicago Stadium was gone. In its place was the brand-new United Center, and Michael had problems shooting there. First he thought the rims were too tight. Then it was the lighting. Then the floor was too slippery. Finally he thought it was the background that was no good. Then one day his old mentor, Tex Winter, asked him, "How come everybody else is shooting so well here?" Right away Michael knew he'd been deceiving himself. His problem had nothing to do with the physical aspects of the arena; his prob-

> I ought to be as solid as anyone who ever played the game.

---

26 BUILD A CASE FOR YOURSELF

Accept responsibility for determining your own mind-set. It's part of your job. It's called mental toughness. Build a case for yourself. Your level of achievement is tied to the self-concept that you build—performance is a self-fulfilling prophecy. Approach every game in the same workmanlike manner, building solid work habits that will hold you up when the going gets tough.

---

lem was psychological. Because he was away doing the baseball thing, he felt left out of the design process for the arena and the team's transition to it. Once he recognized the source of his problem, he dealt with it, and the rest is history.

As an aging third baseman I confront a number of negative thoughts. Am I too old? Are my reactions still there? What about that line drive that tickled the top of my cap last year? Last season I challenged those thoughts with a simple counterpoint: with my years at the position, I ought to be as solid as anyone who ever played the game. I built myself a case. And I believed in the verdict. And guess what? I had a *great* year. There may have been a few balls I might have reached in my younger days, but I didn't boot a ball all year—and I made two of the greatest plays of my life.

So build yourself a case. Your level of achievement is tied to the self-concept that you build—performance is a self-fulfilling prophecy. So make a good case for yourself.

Make Every Game Important

You want to feel well prepared for every game. And you want to feel as well prepared for the game where you're a 10-point favorite as you do when you're a 10-point underdog. You do this by making every game important, by using the same preparation regimen for every game.

Every habit builds on every other habit. You can practice doing things right or practice doing them wrong. By approaching every game in the same workmanlike manner, you build solid work habits that will hold you up when the going gets tough.

Part of your talent as an athlete is the ability to stimulate and harness emotional energy. It takes practice. You don't want to be overstimulated for some games and understimulated for others. Like with anything else, you have to practice adjusting your mind-set. The best way to do this is to see every game as important. And you want to see every act of every game as important.

Take free throws as an example. A free throw at the end of a game when you have a 10-point lead doesn't seem very important. But a free throw at the end of a game when you're one point behind is critical. You want to approach them with the same mind-set—that each is important—neither one more, nor less. Make the 10-point-lead free throw important. Make the one-point-behind free throw another important free throw, and no more. That way you approach every free throw in exactly the same way.

Approach every game in the same manner. Practice making them all important. You'll find it's the best way to build a winning tradition—a tradition of excellence.

The Magic of Visualization

You've reverse planned your game day. You've taken responsibility for your mind-set and built a case for yourself, establishing a strong self-concept that sets the stage for a high level of achievement. Now we're going to use a simple process of visualization to see and feel the great things you're going to do on the playing field.

What Is Visualization?

Visualization is an extremely simple mental imagery technique. For the athlete, it involves putting yourself in a relaxed state and imagining how you will perform—in positive terms.

Studies confirm that your mind and nervous system can tell very little difference between actual and imagined experience. Between two groups of dart throwers, for instance, there is little or no difference in performance between a group that imagines throwing darts and a group that actually throws the darts. In fact, the group that only imagines the task has a basic advantage, because they can imagine doing it right every time.

Reality is a cruel teacher. The actual dart thrower misses his target and has to come to grips with failure. If his problem is mechanical, he may just continue to practice doing it wrong. If he's not careful, he can wind up reinforcing his bad habits.

> *We want to focus both positive thinking and willpower so we can achieve the maximum benefit.*

Not so in the perfect world of our imagination. Here we can hit the target every time using the perfect technique. It's a synthetic experience, but our mind and nervous system will hardly know the difference. We can easily program positive performance pictures that will become part of our subconscious mind—the same subconscious that is going to help us play the game.

Visualization takes advantage of positive thinking. Positive thinking in any endeavor is a plus, but visualization gives us a way to actually harness positive thinking and put it to work. Ditto for willpower. Willpower is another plus, but again we have to find a way to harness that incredible power. We want to focus both positive thinking and willpower so we can achieve the maximum benefit. Visualization gives us the means to do that. We can put the two together in our imagination and walk away with a new and dynamic performance power.

I used to have trouble hitting volleyball serves. I would tense up and totally choke. Using a simple visualization technique, I reprogrammed myself for success. One year I went through an entire season hitting every serve in—more than three hundred serves over two months. I still felt that little exhilaration as I set up to serve, but there was a brand-new certainty, a freedom from doubt—almost like I was on autopilot. It was great.

Why don't more athletes use visualization?

I wish I knew. It's been a proven technique for more than 50 years. Sometimes the psychologists have made it seem too difficult, and for others it comes across as voodoo. Well, it's not voodoo and it doesn't have to be complicated. We'll keep it Dudley simple. There are numerous books out there that can take you to the graduate school level if you're interested. We'll just do what works.

Let's Visualize

Use your reverse game-day schedule to find two focus times—the first for ten minutes and the second for five minutes. You want the first quiet time to be early in the day and the second to be within a couple of hours of game time. These are two times when you can be completely alone. What you're going to do here is nobody else's business.

In focus time number one we'll use our imagination to define the mission. In focus time number two we'll reinforce the objectives.

Everything will be positive here. We'll think in terms of "eye on the ball" rather than "don't move the head." There are no negatives as we program for optimal performance. Sure, we'll confront obstacles and adversity, but our response will always be positive; we'll always be in control of the situation.

Focus Time Number One

Have a pen and paper handy. You're going to jot down a few things.

Get comfortable. Relax. Lie down if you want to, or sit comfortably.

★ 27 VISUALIZE IT

Focus both positive thinking and willpower to achieve maximum benefit. Visualization is your means to bringing these two together. In focus time number one you define the mission. In focus time number two you reinforce the specific objectives. By uniting positive thinking and willpower in your imagination, you produce a new and dynamic performance power.

Clear your mind of all the hoopla. Just let it go blank, like in algebra class.

Feel your body go limp, like a rag doll. Close your eyes. Let go of all the built-up tension. Relax.

Breathe deeply and slowly. Take 10 of these breaths as you count to 10. 1–2–3–4–5–6–7–8–9–10.

Think about the game. *See and feel* what comes to mind. Jot down your responses.

How bad do you want it?

How will you act?

How will you perform your critical tasks?

What obstacles will you face, and how will you respond to them?

Is there someone you can emulate?

How alert will you be?

Your subconscious is ready to provide the answers.

Sample Results of Focus Time Number One

Your results from focus time number one have defined your mission for you. The process has caused you to think through the game and how you will work your will on it. You've seen and felt all the key components. You've made a few notes.

If a stranger were to view your notes, they might appear nonsensical. But they make perfect sense to you. You've taken advantage of a technique, adopted by the United States military, called visual centering. It's a simple concept—it's easier to "see" than remember. Your notes might look something like this:

Junior Seau

I want it BAD.

Always ready—quick and alert—like an Indian warrior

Feed on crowd noise. Bust their crowd, stadium, heroes, hopes, and dreams.

Hit through tackles.

Beat on number 75.

Hammer running backs.

Blitz! I am unstoppable!

Great hands for interceptions—ball hawk
Streak to block kick—dive!
Be high energy all game long.

Again, the notes don't tell the full story, but they do provide reminders for what you have seen, felt, and visualized.

Focus Time Number Two

Focus time number two occurs within a couple of hours of game time. Because you jotted down your key performance objectives, you don't have to reinvent them for focus time number two—you can read them. Focus time number two can last less than five minutes—but it pays tremendous dividends.

Put yourself back in a relaxed state. Breathe deeply and count to 10. Empty your mind. Slowly read down your list, visualizing what you will see and feel while performing the task. Concentrate. Focus on the task. Visualize success and the feeling of success. Stand up to the fear. "See" and "feel" yourself actually doing the tasks to perfection. Know that you will be at your best—at all times—and that ultimately this is the most you can require of yourself.

Back to the Future

You have journeyed to the future—you've seen it, felt it, and influenced it. Instead of worrying about it or wasting psychic energy getting unduly hyped for it, you can let it come to you. You've made reality a better place.

---

28 EXPERIENCE THE FUTURE

Through the vehicle of visualization, you can journey to the future—see it, feel it, and affect it. Instead of worrying about it or wasting psychic energy getting unduly hyped for it, you can let it come to you. You're ready for takeoff, certain of your ability and free from doubt.

It's like you've conducted all your preflight tests and you're ready for takeoff. You're confident, certain of your ability, and free from doubt. Your teammates pick up on your focus. You look them deeply in the eyes, drawing on their strength, infusing them with your magnetic power.

You can enjoy warm-ups, focusing on the task at hand, executing to perfection. You feel an inner calm. There's no need to blow off steam in warm-ups; you know to save it as a reserve for the contest. You have to do it only when it counts.

The other team looks pretty tough. They always look good in warm-ups. Look at them, running their little intimidation drills. Their band is playing; their wanna-be fans are trying to get inside your head. But it's only a matter of time.

When the whistle blows, you'll be ready, *really* ready.

TRAIN TOUGH CHALLENGE

- Make every game important.

- You've done the work. Accept responsibility for your mind-set.

- You deserve to win. Build a case for yourself.

- Reverse plan your game day. Find gaps for two focus times.

- Use your focus times to get ready, *really* ready.

11

THE CONTEST

★

The greater the difficulty, the greater the glory.

—Cicero

Everybody wants it on game day. The question is, how bad?

Do they want it bad enough to have done the work? Or are they only now getting excited because the band is playing? Have they worked as hard as you have? As smart? Do they know you as well as you know them?

You've done the work. You deserve to win. Your two focus times have you programmed to accomplish your key tasks with a quiet ferocity. Your drive to win will propel you to peak performance, the top gear in your transmission box, that final "click" that only competition can bring out. You're ready for the land where there are no guarantees. If you wanted a guarantee, you'd have bought a lawn mower and kept the receipt.

You're ready now for an altered state of consciousness—the experience for which every athlete strives, the experience that makes the whole effort worthwhile. You're ready to get in the flow.

Pseudointellectual: Life has existential risk.
Train Tough Attitude: Bring it on.

The Psychology of Winning

Because as humans we're attracted to the memorable big plays that occur in sports, we sometimes forget that victories are achieved one effort at a time. Most games are won by a team quietly and efficiently beating the other team in the trenches. It's a question of stopped ground balls, made or missed free throws, or the sureness of tackles. It's a lot of little things. The little things add up, eventually leading to the inevitable big plays that determine the game's outcome. When these little things are obvious, we say a team outplayed its opponent.

In the excitement of the game, it's easy to lose focus on the little things. There's hype, fear, and a flurry of disorienting activity. Fortunately, you've already laid the groundwork for success in this most challenging environment. Now it's time to demonstrate competence on the battleground. Like a three-legged stool that never tips, your winning mentality is supported by three constructs: expectation, readiness, and concentration.

Expectation

A couple of years ago I played in a golf tournament, and I did OK until the 18th hole. I was unprepared for the stress of playing in front of the large crowd that had gathered there. Though I'd played other sports in front of crowds, I had never played golf before a crowd. It was a totally unanticipated experience. I did not do well.

Because I was feeling stress, I interpreted the situation negatively, questioning whether my abilities were up to the task of public scrutiny. It was like playing golf on Mars, where gravity's different and there's no oxygen.

A year later I played in the same tournament, with a similar gallery, and I did fine. I knew what to expect and prepared for it. It was no big deal.

Insofar as is possible, know what to expect. Expect bad calls, dumb luck, and some pain. Don't be surprised to be surprised. Adversity is always going to be there. But, hey, adversity is what we thrive on. It's the difficulties that make it interesting. Cicero had it right—the greater the difficulty, the greater the glory. He must have been great out of bunkers.

Want the other guys to challenge. Expect their best shot.

Ferdinand Foch, a French field marshal, had the right attitude during a dicey situation in World War I when he announced: "My center is giving way; my right is in retreat; the situation is excellent. I shall attack!"

Expect that you will respond positively to challenge. Act as if you are equal to any occurrence—because you are. Be resilient.

Act *as if*.

Readiness

The U.S. military has a virtual monopoly on the concept of readiness. In everything we do we ask the question, "Are we ready? Are we *really* ready?" We have readiness reports where we try to assess and communicate where we are. We have readiness exercises to test if we can really do what we say we can do. We've got to be ready to fight and win; that's why you're paying us the big bucks.

It's also an athlete's job to be ready. You don't have the luxury of being surprised by opportunity; you have to expect it.

I'm hardly an expert on soccer, but it's a sport all four of my kids have played. It doesn't take a World Cup veteran to see that soccer is a be-ready sport. The fullbacks must anticipate worst-case scenarios and take immediate action to intercept scoring opportunities before they fully develop.

But it's the forward positions I love. A forward is going to have maybe a couple of scoring opportunities per game. Whether or not the forward scores will be largely dependent on whether or not he is ready to score when the nanosecond of opportunity presents itself. A good forward is like a hungry shark—always moving, always ready to strike. He can't afford to be surprised by opportunity; in fact, he's a hunter of opportunity. He understands that the psychology of scoring is about always being ready.

It's also your job to be ready, regardless of what sport or position you play. Plan on getting off to a good start. Why would you plan otherwise? You have to go through the start of a game to get to the win, and the start is the very first thing you'll do that counts. Be ready for it.

Concentration

There's lots of good news here. Your focus times have taken care of things. You've already established your level of motivation and seen yourself successfully performing key tasks. You've used practice time to establish rituals that you can rely on in the clutch. Congratulations. Now you can let it happen.

Your mind will be fully attuned to the tasks that matter. Because you've already connected to your competitive desire, you can count on your subconscious to keep you focused on the important things.

Desire drives focus. Although a group of pretty girls might be a distraction during normal times, today you won't even notice the cheerleaders. They're not on your priority list for game day.

Keep your self-talk to a minimum. Most of us have a little voice that tries to tell us how we're doing and how things are going. The little voice expresses fear and doubt, usually leading to distraction and anxiety. When that little voice starts yapping, I have a simple answer: "I'm programmed." And it's true. I've already programmed myself for success, and I really don't need a lot of internal noise. One opponent is enough.

Concentration, on the other hand, is a beautiful thing. It's non-judgmental. If an error is made, the focused mind moves easily to the next task, without recrimination. Focus feels good. It knows no fear. And it does *great* work.

When the little voice is quiet and concern about results has ceased, you will find yourself *in the zone*, that place every athlete dreams about. You're taking care of business, and you can accept yourself and your performance as they are. You're doing your best, and you're at your best. What else is there, really?

29 LASER FOCUS

Know what to expect. Be ready for those nanoseconds of opportunity. Let your desire drive focus. Focus knows no fear. It's nonjudgmental. Focus takes you to the zone, that place every athlete dreams about. When you're taking care of business you can accept yourself and your performance for what they are. You're doing your best, and you're at your best. It doesn't get any better.

Dealing with Situations

Stuff happens. A lot of stuff happens—that's what makes a game interesting. That's why people watch games; that's why people play games. Beyond the team-versus-team competition, there are a number of situations and circumstances taking place throughout a game. Some of these things you can influence, but you can't *control* any of them.

Adaptability and resilience are key. Once something's gone wrong, the only thing to do is deal with it. The weather, the crowd, officials, pain and injuries, and dumb luck produce a multitude of situations with which you must deal. By developing and maintaining a healthy attitude about these situations, you can use them to your advantage.

The Weather

Extreme heat, extreme cold, wind, rain, snow, sleet—if the mail carrier always delivers, so can you.

Get into the weather. Have a regimen for every extremity of the year. Experiment with special gear; glory in the insanity of the extreme.

Wouldn't it be great to be a golfer who was especially good in wind? While all the other golfers are grousing around, you're playing low shots to perfection.

Bad weather favors the underdogs. Why? Because it narrows advantages, decreasing the gap between competitors. It makes for a lot of upsets. Favorites tend to lose focus on the task at hand when they fixate on the weather.

Embrace adversity. If you're playing in heat, remind yourself of the day you cut 14 lawns in 110-degree heat. If you're playing in cold, think about all those driveways you shoveled the day school was canceled. Convince yourself you're an Eskimo. If you can't get out of it, *get into it*.

You're never playing the weather; you're always using it to your advantage.

The Crowd

A truly supportive, consistent home crowd is a beautiful thing. You can open your sails and catch the enthusiasm and positivity. These crowds are rare. Most crowds are fickle, even home crowds. Most crowds have one or more bones to pick with the home team or coaching staff. As long as things are sailing along perfectly, these feelings remain in the background. But as soon as things get rocky, the issues surface, and all that support goes south. Sometimes it's a subtle deflation; other times it can be downright ugly.

Crowds are crowds, little more than unruly mobs. They lack leadership and are sometimes sprinkled with drunks. Do you really want to rely on the crowd for your emotional support? I don't think so.

Your emotional base has to be deeper. It has to reach beyond the yearnings of the mob and be grounded in the bedrock of your being. At the end of the day the fans can all go home and resume whatever it is they do for a life. But you're invested; your performance makes a difference. It's nice to please the hometown fans, but you had better be playing for something more. The fans can't catch the ball for you.

I often prefer away games. That's where you find out who you really are. There's something about hostility that lights my fire. Shutting up a hostile crowd is one of life's great rewards. At least you know what you're going up against in an away game. You can count on a challenging environment. Hey, take it on.

I wouldn't recommend baiting a crowd, but I wouldn't back down from it either. It's just one more piece of adversity to meet head-on. And we're in the adversity business.

The Officials

Studies show that the biggest advantage the home team enjoys is the effect of the home crowd on the officials. Imagine trying to make objective calls with a screaming mob making suggestions. It's a tough job—be very glad you don't have to do it.

The officials are part of the game, and you have to know how to work them. You generally do that by showing them a modicum of respect. If you can't respect an official, it's probably because you've never officiated. Try it sometime.

What you'll find is that things happen very, very fast. You'll find you spend a lot of your time trying hard not to make really stupid calls. You find that both teams see the game from only their perspective. You'll find their prejudice predicts how they see the outcome of every close play. They always see it their way, even when the play isn't that close. You'll find that it stings to have your integrity and judgment questioned.

> *Lawyers compete for judgments. Judgments are just part of the game for athletes.*

Give the refs some respect. The vast majority just want to make the right call. Forget any previous problems; start with a clean slate. Once respect is established, you can begin working the refs. Working the refs is little more than letting the officials know that you're watching what they're doing and you're concerned about the calls that have gone the other way. The object is not to hack off the refs or show them up. It's to let them know you're watching, to plant that little seed that maybe they owe you one or that the standards they're using might need adjustment—in your favor.

Most of the time you are going to have to adjust to the refs. In the NBA, teams know that different teams of officials call very different games. That's just the way it is. If officials let a lot of things go, you can play rough. If they call every ticky-tacky thing, you had better adjust accordingly.

You might as well count on some incredibly stupid calls. Some will go your way, and some won't. It'll often feel like you're getting screwed. Chances are, you're not—and it's counterproductive to waste a lot of energy stewing about it.

The surest sign of a team in trouble is when things sour with the refs to the point where the problems become an obsession. When a team is frustrated, the officiating can become the primary target. And that's when the officials beat you. You've let them take over your mind, and your opponent gets a free ride.

Occasionally a coach will have himself ejected to try and change the climate for his team, hoping to wake them up. It's a radical technique, but it sometimes works.

When a player goes off to the point of getting thrown out, it's usually an overreaction to game pressure. The player subconsciously wants out, and getting thrown out is dramatic and final. It's essentially an act of cowardice, disguised as machismo.

Life isn't fair. If you're really concerned about winning judgments, you'd probably make a good lawyer. Lawyers compete for judgments. Judgments are just part of the game for athletes. We can devote a small part of our energy to influencing those judgments, but the focus had better be on the game.

Pain and Injury

I took up racquetball for a brief period. It was a game I found uniquely suited to my reaction and gamesmanship skills. But I made the mistake of playing with animals. I was always getting zinged by the ball, and my free-swinging buddies made me nervous with those rackets whizzing by my face. My back bothered me after I played. I was a racquetball sissy.

So I quit. I just up and quit and never looked back.

I respect racquetball players, and I think it's a great game, but racquetball offered a type of fear and pain I hadn't grown up with, and it wasn't for me. I could take a hit in football and watch a fastball skim my chest, but that racquetball court was scary.

You have to have a tolerance for the danger and pain that come with your sport. It's another mind-over-matter challenge. You have to play with abandon. You can't be thinking about getting hit. It's one of those things you build into your focus time sessions—abandon.

> *Those play-hurt periods can show us a lot about ourselves.*

It's interesting how different individuals respond to pain. For some guys it's always a big deal, with a lot of special effects and drama, as if they need attention. It gets tiresome. Pretty soon teammates and coaches learn to ignore the whole show. It's always the same guys stopping play while they act like they just had a leg amputated.

Other guys just take the pain and move on. You never know they're hurting.

Football taught me to take inventory when I get my bell rung. I ask myself, "Is it serious, or does it just hurt?" Most of the time it's something I can tolerate and play through. No use making a fuss. On the other hand, if you have something that needs attending to, that's going to make you a liability for a couple of plays, get the heck off the field. The more serious injuries are obvious, and it's probably time for a doctor's advice. Just don't go into a dramatic seizure every time something hurts.

Playing with injury or illness is a special calling. There may be times when you still have to go when you're only 75 percent or you've got the flu. Those situations can do marvelous things for your focus. The mental part of your game steps up and becomes stronger to compensate for the physical handicap. That's why many guys coming off an injury never miss a beat. They've worked their visualization skills into overdrive, their focus and concentration more than making up for the physical shortfall.

Those play-hurt periods can show us a lot about ourselves—not only that we have the guts to tough it out, but the incredible value of that little bit of extra focus and preparation. It's a lesson we can carry over to when we're 100 percent healthy.

Lady Luck

In the 1999 NBA playoffs, the New York Knicks' Allan Houston drove the lane and lofted an ugly floater that bounced high off the right side of the rim, hit the backboard, and rattled in. It gave the Knicks a one-point victory and eliminated the Miami Heat from the playoffs. It's rare that a shot that hits the rim that far off the mark goes in. Some would call it dumb luck.

But was it?

The Knicks had taken the Heat to the deciding game. There was a one-point difference in the score. Houston had the guts to drive the lane and take the last shot, and he had the presence of mind to get the ball up over the rim where it had a chance to go in. The replay also showed that the shot came as a result of a carefully crafted play designed by Coach Jeff Van Gundy. Sure the bounce was lucky, but seen in context, it was just a small part of a much larger scheme.

It's rare when an entire series comes down to the lucky bounce of a ball. But Lady Luck is always out there flashing her smile, trying to be noticed. She's a fickle, mystifying force. And to those who pay her too much attention, she is a frequent distraction. She seems to respond best to those who play hardest, who disregard her frequent mood swings and focus on doing all the little things that winning demands. She usually goes home with the team that wows her.

Yes, it's better to be lucky than good. But you usually get lucky by being good.

So don't let luck become something you focus on. Focus instead on taking care of business, and the luck thing will take care of itself.

Have I said that enough ways?

Riding the Pine

For every guy on the field there are two guys sitting on the bench, and some of those guys are scheduled to sit there for a very long time.

From sixth grade to the pros, it's the same story: a lot of guys riding the pine. It's one of the very worst things about sports.

Imagine being an NBA benchwarmer. To get to that exclusive piece of pine, you were probably the very best player on your high school and college team. You were a star. Now you're an NBA also-ran, with little or no experience riding the pine.

I took a college course in pine riding and graduated summa cum laude in the experience. For two solid years, I rode pine for the Wheaton College baseball team, a truly humiliating experience. I carried the bats, chased foul balls, and kept score. For two years I was never judged competent to pinch hit, pinch run, or play a half-inning of defense. This was a team that played all doubleheaders. It was tough.

I was strong enough to stay on the team and eventually break into the lineup by my junior year. But it was still a regime that I never felt had confidence in my abilities, and it even caused me to doubt myself. It's tough to keep the right picture of yourself when the environment isn't right, when the system, for whatever reason, is treating you like a second-class citizen. I don't dwell on the situation, but I learned a lot from it. I know what it's like in a funky karma.

Keep a business mentality. Be ready.

There's a three-step process I recommend when you see a bench-warming situation on your horizon: *avoid, avoid, avoid.* I'd rather have playing time at Podunk U than sit on the bench at Notre Dame. It's your call, but let me tell you, bench time is tough. Avoid when possible.

If you do get stuck there, devise a plan to get off. Be ready to go. The bench is no place for daydreaming, making friends, or feeling sorry for yourself. Your sole purpose in life is to be ready to go in and do good things in strange situations. Don't let the situation paint your picture for you. Keep a business mentality. Be ready. Find a perspective from which you can stay motivated. You never know when you might get your chance.

How'd you like to have been Mickey Mantle's backup? For three years in the early '60s that man was Jack Reed. Jack was a good outfielder, but he was just a so-so hitter without much power. What playing time he got came in the late innings if Mickey's knees were bothering him. It was a big shadow to play under.

My dad worked with a lot of Yankees over his career, and one Sunday in Detroit he noticed that Jack seemed a little down. Dad is a master psyche artist, and he started pumping Jack up, praising all the little things he saw Jack doing and telling him the things that bench jockeys so seldom hear. We wound up taking Jack to church before the game, dropping him off just in time to catch the team bus.

> *Riding the pine is tough and demoralizing, but the rewards of coming off the bench can be worth the wait.*

We were in for a long day. The game, played on June 24, 1962, went 13 extra innings, one of the longest baseball games ever played. The game was broken up in the 22nd inning with a three-run shot from a little-known backup named Jack Reed.

It was a great object lesson in what pumping a little sunshine into a guy could do. Jack was ready that day; his blast got everybody home by midnight. He hit only one home run in his big-league career, but he hit it in the spotlight.

Riding the pine is tough and demoralizing, but the rewards of coming off the bench can be worth the wait.

Scott Wedman was an NBA All-Star forward who had a 13-year NBA career. He spent the last years of it with the Boston Celtics playing behind Larry Bird, who won three MVP awards during that period.

Scott lives down the street from me. I once hit a nine iron off my front lawn, and the shot landed on his roof. I often see Scott out walking his dogs, so I'm always pestering him about some piece of Celtic lore.

Scott admits to having difficulty adjusting to a backup role, that it required sacrificing ego and looking for new places to contribute.

"Mentally it was a lot more difficult," Scott told me, "not knowing whether or not I'd play. It's easy to feel sorry for yourself. You come of the bench without warm-ups, knowing that with a couple mistakes you'll be off again. The key for me was to stay ready and enthusiastic and keep my mind involved in the game."

He learned to turn practices into playoff games, battling Bird and staying after practice to challenge Bird one-on-one, but only occasionally beating him.

"Larry had a flair for the dramatic," Scott recalls. "I'd get ahead and he'd come back and beat me. I had him down 7–2 one time in a game to 11, then some news cameras appeared. 'You're in trouble now,' Bird warned me—and of course he came back to win."

Scott Wedman's hard work and always-ready philosophy paid off.

> *Be consistent.*
> *Stay in the moment.*
> *Focus on the job at hand.*

He became a solid contributor, effectively spelling key players during long periods of injury as well as turning games around in shorter stints of play.

In the '84 NBA Finals he hit a game-winning baseline jumper against the Los Angeles Lakers to knot the series at 1–1—a brutal series the Celtics would eventually win in seven games.

But it was in the NBA Finals a year later against the same Los Angeles Lakers that the name Scott Wedman became a part of the basketball record books. In what was dubbed the "Memorial Day Massacre," Wedman went on an incredible 11 for 11 shooting spree that remains an NBA Finals record to this day.

I asked Scott about his mind-set that day.

"By that time, I was very methodical in my game preparation," he told me, "I used pregame visualization to see myself performing my critical tasks and roles. I had a good focus going in."

But it was the play of teammate Danny Ainge that inspired Wedman to go to the next level.

"Danny got hot," Scott recalled, "and I was just so thrilled for him. His play inspired me, and I caught the same focused, carefree attitude where we just threw all caution to the wind."

Riding the pine is tough. But there's nothing like coming off the bench and straight into the record books for curing the blahs.

It's a Long Game

Every game is unique. Each game has its own twists and turns, ups and downs, and an infinite array of variables. Most games have clearly discernable waves of momentum, with the advantage shifting from team to team. Like a surfer, your object is to ride your team's positive waves all the way to the beach. And conversely, you want to find ways to upset your opponents' rhythm when things are going their way.

Realize that it's a long game and that there are naturally going to be swings of momentum between teams. There are very few perfect games; there are usually plenty of opportunities to blame yourself or others, lose faith, become overconfident, or quit.

Don't let the swings of fortune get to you. You can't be as effective if you're bouncing between highs and lows with every bounce of the ball.

Be consistent. Stay in the moment. Focus on the job at hand. Trust that your pregame focus times will allow you to perform at your best if you stay on task.

Expect to be resilient, to be able to bounce back from adversity. Regardless of how you've performed earlier in the game, there is always the opportunity for redemption at the end. As Yogi said, "It ain't over 'til it's over."

Because it's a long game you need to pick your spots to actually rest and catch your breath. Find ways to conserve energy between the action. Use time-outs to sit and relax. And halftime is not for wimps, it's a time to completely chill out. Conserve energy where you can in order to have it when you need it.

Feed off teammates; they are a valuable source of psychological fuel. Look them in the eyes and charge your batteries. Keep a positive outlook. It's going to be a long game.

Get Off to a Good Start

This seems self-evident, but a lot of teams spot their opponents a free advantage by starting poorly. Eventually, it catches up with them.

> ## 30 UNDERSTAND MOMENTUM
>
> Most games have waves of momentum, with the advantage shifting from team to team. Your objective is to ride your team's positive waves all the way to the beach. And conversely, you must find ways to upset your opponents' rhythm when things are going their way. Start the game strong. When ahead, keep the pressure on. When the going gets tough, attack! Staging a comeback is like starting a fire. It begins with a spark, flickers a bit, ignites, begins burning, requires stoking, and then builds so much heat that it consumes everything in its path.

Start the game strong. Make it a habit. Sure, there's time to make up for a bad start—but what's the point in that? When the game starts, it's time to play. Period.

The starts of the second half and fourth quarter also yield bonus points. There's something about the start of those periods that sets the tone for what's to come.

Set the tone by coming out of the chute strong.

When You're Ahead

I'd rather be ahead than behind, but it's close.

There are few things worse than overconfidence, and there's nothing worse than thinking you've got a game won only to walk into an ambush.

There's only one way to handle being ahead, and that's to keep the pressure on. There may be a leadership decision to play more conservatively, but you must keep the pressure on. That means getting men on base, extending pitch counts, hitting free throws, making hard tackles—in short, doing all the little things you're supposed to do. The problem is, it's easy to stop doing all those little things if you get complacent.

Success breeds euphoria, and the euphoric are easy pickings. Any lieutenant worth his salt knows that his unit is most vulnerable right after they've taken the hill. In World War I the Germans made a science out of counterattacking every time the French broke through the line.

I have a saying for baseball players when the team is ahead in the late innings: "squeeze the easy ones." Most teams that blow leads have a hand in their own downfall. Someone, or a bunch of someones, fails to accomplish the routine. If you can keep squeezing the easy ones, under pressure, you have a much better chance of making the tough plays as well.

> *The game's going to play itself out, and you better be playing as long as there's game left to play.*

And it's the same in every sport. It's making blocks and tackles in football. Hitting the ball over the net in tennis. Hitting free throws in basketball. Serving the ball in play in volleyball. They're all things that should be routine but that sometimes get forgotten when we get complacent.

The problem with complacency is that it sets the stage for panic. One minute you're rolling along feeling good about things, and the next minute you're feeling the pinch. Panic is like cancer—it's best dealt with early. Take a deep breath and get refocused. Slow down; take a time-out if necessary. Teams with a lead often start rushing, as if that will somehow shorten the game. It doesn't. The game's going to play itself out, and you better be playing as long as there's game left to play.

Put a hand up and lead. Get back to performing. It's a long game.

When You're Behind

You're behind. So what?

How you got there is in the past. Forget about it.

For those who remain calm and refuse to quit, there will be golden opportunities to turn the worm.

Momentum has been known to change jerseys. Chances are someone has sprung a comeback even crazier than the one you're planning.

Much of what you need to do is the same stuff you do to get ahead—or stay ahead. Perform the fundamentals.

But now you're also looking to spring an ambush. You're hoping to create havoc and catch the bad guys off guard. Maybe you can exploit that little bit of fear they carry around in their chests. Maybe you can get them to help you.

You're going to have to take some chances. What have you got to lose?

Staging a comeback is like starting a fire. It begins with a tiny spark, flickers a little bit, ignites, begins burning, requires stoking, and then builds so much heat that it consumes everything in its path. Somebody's got to provide the spark. Somebody's got to do something to build on it. Then the whole team has got to catch the fire and bring it to bear on the enemy. You want to be a player with sparks flying off you. You want your team to be a living, breathing tinderbox, always ready to catch fire. Good teams know how to explode. It's part of who they are. There is no fun like a successful comeback. There's absolutely nothing like it.

> *Good teams understand the psychology of the comeback. Great teams actually prepare for it.*

Good teams understand the psychology of a comeback. Great teams actually prepare for it.

The psychology of the comeback is best understood in what I call "the baboon effect." It's a phenomenon I observed 20 years ago at the San Diego Zoo and have used to great advantage ever since. The zoo had a large family of baboons living in a habitat. There were mom and dad baboons, grandparents, babies, and "teens." As in most animal cultures, it was in the teen set where the action occurred. One teen baboon would chase another teen baboon looking to whup his butt. This would continue until the chasee turned and faced his pursuer, bared his fangs, and stood his ground. At that point, the chasee became the pursuer. This ritual went back and forth ad infinitum. I could see the whole psychology of winning and losing played out among those crazy baboons.

Opossums are also interesting. An opossum will feign death when confronted by certain natural enemies. While feigning death is not a particularly useful technique on a sports field, it does have its place. I've used it in volleyball. Volleyball is a great sport to look for momentum swings. There are always a lot of them. Volleyball emotion can be charted on a scale of 1 to 10, with 10 being sky-high and 1 being dead in the water. You usually want your team starting a match at about a 7. That means they're fired up, but they still have room to grow. Suppose the team starts at 7 and falls behind. They try to ramp up to a 10 but hit a brick wall and lose the first two games. Maybe all the enthusiasm is getting in the way. Maybe it's time to take advantage of the baboon effect by playing possum.

It's a radical action. It's something the team must understand and practice before the match. It might work once a season. Playing possum requires completely letting go of results and ramping down emotion to a 2. It means feigning death to the opponent. The team focuses only on fundamentals and shows no emotional response to success or failure. The other team concludes you've given up. Inevitably you creep back into the match. On the leader's signal, when the moment is right to wreak maximum havoc, the team explodes to an emotional 10, and the ambush is sprung. The other guys are running like a teenage baboon and have no idea why. If they stop to fight, you just whup the hell out of them.

Breeding opossums with baboons is clearly advanced animal husbandry. But you get the idea.

When the going gets tough, take a deep breath, stop the bleeding, and attack!

Game Mantras

Athletes speak in code. We communicate by means of whistles, hand signals, and body language. Because we perform in an action arena, there isn't always time for a full explanation. "X1 flare-out on three" is about all we need. Everyone can take his cue from one simple play call.

Jocks sometimes get the reputation for being shallow, as though we live our lives through a series of grunts and groans. Well, we do. We have to reduce things to their lowest common denominator and get to the point. There isn't time for a lot of sermonizing. Still, we need to find motivation like anyone else. We're always looking for something to grab on to, some way of thinking about the effort that will keep us focused and charged up. A good mantra fills the bill.

"Win one for the Gipper" is the classic example. Teams will dedicate an effort to someone, maybe a deceased teammate or a handicapped child. It gives players a new perspective and something larger to play for. During World War II the Navy Midshipmen football team was reminded that submarines were surfacing and risking their lives just so the sailors could listen to the Army-Navy game. No pressure, they were told, but maybe you could make it worth their while.

A good mantra will provoke superhuman effort. Football creates a lot of great mantras—simple thoughts to carry into a contest where the going will be tough. Here are two of my favorites:

Whatever It Takes

Adopted by the Pittsburgh Steelers, the motto "whatever it takes" kept their heads screwed on and helped motivate them to four Super Bowl Championships.

It's a great attitude going into a season or a game. It's the attitude of endless effort, regardless of circumstances, and of the will to carry on the battle no matter what the requirements.

Find a Way to Win

Bill Parcells has had success wherever he's coached in the NFL, and part of his success is his ability to communicate his "find a way to win" philosophy.

A team's ultimate success in the NFL often boils down to its ability to win the close games, to win even when having an otherwise bad day. "Find a way to win" keeps everything focused on creative pursuit of the win. The focus here is on keeping everything keyed to creativity in pursuit of victory. If the offense is sputtering and the defense is porous, maybe the specialty teams will have to carry the day. Maybe one guy will have to step up and make the play of his life. Maybe that guy is you.

With the whole team focused on finding a way to win, anything is possible. The point is to be mentally prepared for close games and the moments that determine victory or defeat. Those moments will be the subject of our next chapter. It's crunch time.

TRAIN TOUGH CHALLENGE

- Expect adversity. Expect bad calls, dumb luck, and some pain. Maintain a healthy attitude about situations.

- Be ready for opportunity, not surprised by opportunity. It's a matter of nanoseconds.

- Play the *entire* game; ride the waves of momentum, and keep the pressure on your opponent.

- When the going gets tough, take a deep breath, stop the bleeding, and attack!

12

CRUNCH TIME

★

There is a time to take counsel of your fears, and there is a time to never listen to any fear.

—General George S. Patton

The mother cheetah has hunted gazelles for a week without result. Her cubs are starving, and she is weakened from a lack of nourishment and a drought that has dried up the water holes in the savanna. She has strength for just one more hunt—one more exhausting chase.

Cheetahs are genetically programmed to hunt, with lessons passed silently along from generation to generation. But cheetahs also learn from their own hunting experience and the mistakes made in hunts where dinner got away.

This last hunt is life or death; the cheetah will not have strength enough or speed enough for another try. A gazelle can motor at 70 miles per hour, and it too faces life or death and will be driven by a motivating fear and the instinctual knowledge that bad things happen when the race is lost.

The cheetah hunts with a new focus. Gone is the sloppiness exhibited earlier in the week. She positions herself more carefully now, creeping with a stealth and patience we have not seen before. This time, she chooses the perfect moment to spring. This time, her chase is more intense, her drive is all out. It's crunch time.

This time she runs through the gazelle, taking it down in a murderous rage, breaking its neck with her powerful jaws. The cheetah is motivated by hunger, yet unencumbered by the fear of failure. Her actions are instinctual, unfettered by the little voice that comes with human consciousness. Crunch time for the cheetah is loaded with pluses; her motivation is complete; she performs without the burden of a single negative thought.

Why can't humans perform in the same way? Why do we see such wildly divergent performance with the game on the line? How can we get ready for crunch time?

Typical Jock: Shouldn't Joe take the last shot?
Train Tough Attitude: Let me take care of it.

Understanding Negativity at Crunch Time

I want to use this section to get out all the negativity that comes with crunch time. We'll just get it right out in the open and be done with it. No use hiding it, people choke. Just when we most need to perform, we tighten up and the cause is lost.

Like many athletes, I spent a good part of my career with a mediocre performance record at crunch time. I wondered if I really had what it takes or whether there wasn't some secret to getting it done in the clutch.

One instance haunted me for years. I took a pass off a fast break in basketball and laid the ball up with two seconds on the clock. My team was down a point. The ball dribbled out. Mysteriously, a foul was called. I don't remember anybody touching me, but I was awarded two shots. I missed them both. After the second shot, the ball bounced right back in my hands, so there I was with an eight-foot shot to win or lose the game. I missed the shot. That's a total of four missed shots in two seconds, with the game on the line—probably some kind of record. It still hurts when I think about it.

Choking is like a virus, and in basketball I picked it up as a kid and carried it for years. Basketball became the ultimate challenge for me; it's a game I still play to this day. Basketball has taught me that to master crunch time, you have to remain open to learning the right lessons—no matter how painful.

Choking is a learned response to stress, and the behavior is reinforced with every failure. Performance anxiety invariably leads to a loss of athletic form and regression to a lower skill level. Reaction time

There's a time in our lives when there are no boundaries, when we believe we can do anything.

increases, flexibility decreases, and muscular tension leads to early fatigue. Players sweat more, while their heart rate and blood pressure increase. The mouth feels dry, and breathing becomes rapid and shallow—hence the choking effect.

A player in the throes of choking looks and acts differently. There are telltale signs of nervous activity—pacing, wiping, and the jitters. The player hardly knows what to do with himself. He has difficulty processing information because he's worrying about the consequences of failure. The little voice has become a major nuisance. How am I doing? Can I do it? Where can I hide? Fear is taking over. Negative fantasies abound. Movements are strained. Worst of all, focus on the task is lost.

Observe one of the poor saps selected to attempt a field goal for big bucks at the halftime of an NFL game. He's had all day to master his kicking technique with the help of a professional kicking coach. But at crunch time he comes unglued. The subtleties of choking that we sometimes find in professional athletes are showing in spades with this guy. We can see that he's dead meat before he ever gets near the ball. Nothing in his background has prepared him for the pressure of kicking for that much money, in front of that many people. The last time he felt like this was when he forgot his line at the Sunday school Christmas pageant. We're not surprised that his move to the ball looks wooden, that his head comes up, and that he hardly makes contact with the ball. They should hire this guy as an onside kick artist.

And that's the trouble with choking—you can choke from not enough experience or from too much of the wrong kind of experience.

Most acts of heroism in battle take place in a soldier's first day of conflict. After that he knows the consequences for risk taking. Heroism after the first day is courage on another level.

Ever hear of the sophomore jinx? That's when the sophs realize they weren't supposed to be able to do all those things they already did as freshmen. They stop to think of what the consequences would have been had they failed.

Right now I'm drinking coffee from a mug that my son Matt won eight years ago at the Circus-Circus Hotel Casino in Reno, Nevada. It's the only mug I drink out of around the house because it's so special to me. Matt won it when he was four years old by knocking down a bunch of milk bottles with a beanbag. Fifty kids were lined up taking turns throwing the beanbag, and none of them came close to knocking down the bottles. I didn't really want to waste a dollar on the enterprise, but Matt kept insisting it would be easy and that he could do it—and to my great surprise, he did.

> *Michael Jordan is a great pressure player* because *of his willingness to shoulder failure.*

The next summer, just after he turned five, he won 10 dollars from his Uncle Tom by hitting eight shots in a row on the basketball court. Actually, he hit ten in a row, but the bet was for eight.

There's a time in our lives when there are no boundaries, when we believe we can do anything. Then we inevitably bump up against reality, and we have to learn how to deal with it. Perfection will not be an option. Excellence is attainable, but those who insist on a tidy battlefield are in for a rude awakening. It takes a healthy self-image to persevere through the inevitable setbacks and, yes, failures.

The same Michael Jordan who was cut from his high school basketball team became the greatest player ever to play the game. Not only that, he became the greatest clutch player ever to play the game. Nobody was better than Michael Jordan in the clutch. Nobody wanted the ball at crunch time more than Jordan, and he had a sixth sense about those around him. He knew whom to trust at crunch time.

Jordan was always willing to risk failure, one of the keys to crunch time. The "risk-averse" are usually looking the other way at crunch time. You've got to be willing to accept the responsibility of failure to be effective with the game on the line.

Jordan had many notable failures. He played poorly down the stretch of several playoff games to end the Bulls' season in 1995. His last-second shot caromed off the rim in game five against the Jazz in 1998—a shot that would have won the championship for the Bulls right then and there. Jordan missed the game-winning shot many times over his career. But he always came back for more.

We celebrate Michael Jordan as a great pressure player despite his failures. In fact, Michael Jordan is a great pressure player *because* of his willingness to shoulder failure.

But enough about failure. I think we've established the major challenges of crunch time. And we're not going to dwell on them. In the next section we'll rebuild your attitude about crunch time, focusing only on the positive. Let the negativity pass like a kidney stone. If you own this book, take a marker and just cross out this entire section. It's time to move on.

Crunch-Time Secrets

As in any human endeavor, it's important to know where you are. The key to mastering a task is honestly assessing how you've done in the past so you can tweak a few things and get to the master level.

Does your performance at crunch time ramp up, or do you close down?

Are you better in practice, or do you peak when the game's on the line?

Coming through at crunch time is more than a wheel of chance. If you pay attention, you can get a good read on yourself. Then, you can reinforce the good things you're doing and fix any problems you're having.

Coming through at crunch time is challenging—that's why the rewards are so great. For years, I wondered what the secret was. By experiencing and observing my own reactions in the clutch, I eventually figured it out. Crunch time is now money time. Gone is the anxiety I used to carry in my rucksack.

The secrets revealed themselves. Not surprisingly, they fit quite nicely with the Train Tough strategies we've established so far. You're ready now for the crunch-time secrets.

Plan on Crunch Time

It's important to understand how critical crunch time is, but the time to deal with all that is before the game. You don't want it dawning on you for the first time as you stand over the critical putt.

Plan on crunch time. It's going to happen. You're going to be ready.

You've already thought through crunch time during your focus times. You've front-end loaded your burning desire and put it to good use. "Front-end loading" means taking the importance of an upcoming game and using it to motivate preparation, not just performance in the game itself. It's like an investment. Invest early, and reap the dividends later. Then you can trust yourself to take care of business during the game. You won't be surprised by crunch time.

By crunch time, the yearnings of the crowd, the hopes and dreams of alumni, and the hype of the media are all a footnote to the task at hand. What they think, do, or say has no impact on your focus. It's almost as though they're the enemy, a bunch of screaming wanna-bes who look for a life in what you're about to do.

Front-end load all the magnitude stuff. Sure the game is important. But the time to realize that is before it starts, so you can relax and be ready for action at crunch time.

Act As If

Here's where we demonstrate character. Here's where we act through fear. This is where we live out a word called *courage*.

Remember, it's your job to perform in the clutch. Seriously, it's in your job description. Right here: "performs in clutch." It's not some excruciating torture that you have to live through at the end of the game. It's what you do. It's why you're here.

The fact that you are an athlete is in itself an act of courage. It says that you are willing to risk failure. All the people who dropped out along the way and are spending their lives watching TV and playing video games have not lived up to that standard. And you aim to exceed the standard.

You risk failure just by being out there. But you must do more than that—you must actively risk failure. It's not enough to just be there.

You must act, and act with supreme confidence. It goes back to the matador walk. It's stepping up to the plate like you just hit 10 home runs and have a ticket in your pocket for number 11.

Act *as if* you expect to win.

Act *as if* you're a winner.

Believe in yourself. Act *as if*.

Commit to Coming Through

I play pickup basketball three times a week at Ft. Leavenworth, Kansas, usually with active-duty soldiers half my age. It's taught me a lot about crunch time. We normally play four or five full-court games to 11, so there are four or five game-winning shots every time we play. For the longest time I would lay off taking these shots, letting one of the younger guys have the lead. That was before I built confidence in my jump shot. Over time I realized I was a high-percentage shooter who ought to be taking that last shot.

I got to where I would *take* the last shot. But that wasn't good enough. I had to commit to *make* the last shot. The guts to take the last shot is only a preliminary step; you have to commit to making it.

The very first step in the process is identifying the winning shot. By that I mean consciously realizing the count is at 10 and the next basket is the winner. Then you consciously say to yourself, "I'm going to make the next shot."

It's as simple as that. You recognize the situation and commit to coming through.

---

31 PLAN ON CRUNCH TIME

It's going to happen. You need to be ready. Consciously identify crunch-time moments, and commit to coming through. That way you're primed for success instead of being surprised by opportunity. Crunch time is what we dream about. Be ready for it.

If somebody else takes the shot, that's fine. You were ready to hit the shot if your number came up.

Some will say it's better to just stay in the flow of the game and treat the last shot like any other shot. That's true—and there are times when you're so into the flow of the game that you perform right through the game winner. But the reality is that the game shot is different. It's different because the nature of the game makes it different. The game shot draws the spotlight—always has, always will. There's no ignoring it. Might as well plan for it, act through it, and commit to knocking it down.

This technique holds true for every sport with a crunch time. It might be, "I'm going to make this putt . . . catch the ball . . . or . . . tackle the ball carrier."

The point is to commit to coming through—at crunch time.

Stay in the Moment

Let's stay with the basketball illustration and build to the proverbial "game-on-the-line" free throw. You're shooting two—the first to tie, the second to win. The opposing coach calls time-out; he wants to "ice" you.

There are several reasons why he will be unsuccessful.

First of all, you've front-end loaded all the magnitude stuff. You knew how important the game was during your focus times; you prepared for this moment *before* the game began.

Second, you're acting *as if*. Every move you make radiates confidence. You've got the bad guys right where you want them.

---

32 STAY IN THE MOMENT

It's not enough to be there, you have to be all the way there. You've front-end loaded all the magnitude stuff. You're radiating confidence. You know it's crunch time, and you've committed to coming through. So *be* where you are in the process. *Stay in the moment.*

Third, you know it's crunch time, and you consciously commit to making the shots.

Now all you have to do is stay in the moment.

The actual act of shooting a free throw, from the trigger movement to the release of the ball, is about 1.5 seconds. Because you're shooting two free throws in this example, your actual work time is about three seconds. The rest is all get-ready or follow-through.

The point is that the time spent actually shooting the free throws is finite, but the time leading up to each shot is important too. You can't shoot the shot in advance of being handed the ball; you can shoot only after you're handed the ball.

So what should you do with all the extra time? Stay in the moment. Be where you are in the process. In fact, you have to be all the way there. Listen to what the coach says in the huddle. Really listen. Feed off your teammates. Look them in the eyes. Radiate confidence. Execute your preshot regimen exactly as you practiced it.

Make the shot. Stay in the moment. Make the shot.

Take the rest of the day off.

TRAIN TOUGH CHALLENGE

- Plan for crunch time. It's going to happen. Front-end load all the magnitude stuff, so you use the importance of the game as a motivator first for preparation, and then for game performance.

- Act *as if*. It's in your job description. It's why you're here.

- Recognize the crunch-time moment. Commit to coming through.

- Stay in the moment. Wherever you are in the process of preparing—be there.

PART FOUR

FACE THE NEW WORLD
UNDERSTAND THE PAST, DOMINATE THE PRESENT, SERIOUSLY IMPACT THE FUTURE

13

UNDERSTAND THE ARENA

★

The truth of the matter is that you always know the right thing to do. The hard part is doing it.
—GENERAL NORMAN SCHWARZKOPF

Sports are not inherently good.

I know that sounds radical, so let me say it again: sports are not inherently good.

Since the end of World War II the world has gone sports mad. The time and money spent on sports has gone off the chart.

It wasn't always that way. Time was in this country when sports were largely regarded as a waste of time—much as many of us regard video games and TV today. My grandfather was thrown out of the house at age 16 for playing in a baseball game. In the 1920s and '30s work came first. Ball playing was a distraction.

In the '50s there were still guys who turned down major league baseball careers because they wouldn't play ball on Sunday. You could still find towns where ball diamonds, tennis courts, and beaches were closed on Sunday.

Loser Focus: Did you see Jerry Springer last night?
Train Tough Attitude: Let's head for the gym.

Are We Ancient Rome?

Today the preacher better get the service done on time so we don't miss an NFL kickoff. More than likely, junior has a game scheduled during the 10:00 service.

The corporate sports world has really got it going on. Fans have bought into just about everything, and I do mean *bought*. The prices we pay to be fans are astronomical. And we can't get enough of it. We're buying in to teams that move, players that get traded or become free agents, and facilities that are named after corporations. It's crazy, and there's no end in sight.

We look a lot like ancient Rome. We certainly share the same need for distraction and entertainment, and pro wrestling certainly gets us close. But so far we're just simulating.

Still, you only have to visit a kids' soccer game to see that something's out of whack. The screaming parents tell the story. Johnny's going to overcome the odds and be the one kid to bring soccer into the mainstream of American sports. He's going to be that great. Fred Engh's *Why Johnny Hates Sports* tells the story—we've made junior's performance on the athletic field a focal point for all the other shortcomings in the family. Sports have gotten into everything.

And we've got everything into sports. The spectacle of the Olympics is overshadowed by the scandals of the international leadership and of athletes who blood dope and use steroids and hormones. You can blow all the trumpets you want—light as many torches as you want—when you peel back the veneer, it's an ugly sight. The Olympic ideal is admirable; the reality is not.

The Arena's Ugly—You Don't Have to Be

When you take the field you had better be ready for reality. And reality is always ugly. Forget about the halftime show. Don't even look at the cheerleaders. From Little League to Major League, it's a jungle.

Remember, sports mirror life. In fact, it's worse than that—sports mirror the toughest part of life—the competitive part. That's why I say it's a jungle. You hunt; you're hunted. You win; you lose. A lot of heavy stuff happens in between. Don't kid yourself. Understand the system.

You think I'm wolfing you?

What about the "beauty" of sports, you say?

What about figure skating, you say?

Read Christine Brennan's *The Edge of Glory*, and you'll find out how beautiful figure skating is. Figure skating is beautiful for about two minutes of ice time . . . if you don't wipe out. The rest is a rat race, Baby, with real rats. Remember Tonya Harding's signature move on Nancy Kerrigan? I'd rather play hockey.

Understand the system. Then be your own person. Decide whom you want to be out there. Do you want to be a good guy? Or a bad guy? What actions are acceptable to you? Where do you draw the line?

My advice to you is to take the high road, whenever one presents itself. Just don't be naive about the system. Understand it. Read on, and we'll talk about how to dominate it.

Women in the Arena

Women are finding sports in increasing numbers. We can be proud that the United States leads the way in this social phenomenon. Women need sports just as men do, and now opportunities are opening up everywhere.

---

33 UNDERSTAND THE SYSTEM

Sports mirror life. In fact, sports mirror the ugliest part of life. You hunt; you're hunted. You win; you lose. And a lot of heavy stuff happens in between. It's a jungle. Decide who you want to be out there. Do you want to be a good guy? Or a bad guy? What actions are acceptable to you? Where do you draw the line? Don't kid yourself. Understand the system.

Still, the sports world is a male-dominated culture. The sports that capture the public imagination are those where men have a physical advantage. Money drives the train. Where the fans go, the money goes; athletes are ultimately drawn to sports where they have the opportunity for a professional career.

Women are catching up; in fact, in sports that place a premium on flexibility and balance, they have always had the lead. The culture just doesn't pay attention. Women have an inherently superior sense of team; they bond better than men do. We use the term "male bonding" as if it's something special, because bonding is a difficult task for men.

Rare is the man who hasn't experienced the new woman athlete. I know I have, and it's a unique sensation—especially on my old stomping ground, the basketball court. It's a new world.

My female teammates in volleyball are phenomenal. They routinely put in what I call "perfect games." That's playing an entire game without a single error. That's every serve in, every set and bump on target, not a miss or a net ball. When women have access to quality programs, the results are eye-opening.

The Nature of Sports

Understand the nature of sports. Sports are part of nature. Even the animals play—it's how they learn to problem solve. Kids are the same way. Ever notice how they're into everything, exploring, and screwing up? It's how they learn.

I want to fight 'em off, tooth and nail.

We're genetically programmed to play. We're also programmed to stop playing as we age. That's why adults can be so boring.

Sports are a paradigm for what goes on in the animal kingdom. Remember, we are animals. Take a pride of lions. The dominant male rules. He's got his pick of the females and he's first in line for chow. He fends off the competition as long as he can. Eventually, a stronger lion drives him off. The new dominant male kills the first lion's offspring. It's that bad.

Now I know why I'm picking up some hostility in the gym. I can feel the young bloods closing in. I want to fight 'em off, tooth and nail. It's an animal reaction. Plus, I remember how I was at that age.

Now I've got my own sons. The two oldest are beating me in arm wrestling. But, hey, I'm working on a comeback.

Burn Up Aggression

Whether it's the irritability of an old grouch or the seething rage of a testosterone-laden teenager, we all have an aggression instinct. Since we killed off the mastodons a while back and saber-toothed tigers no longer roam the land, we need something to give us the same jolt. War is always around, and that seems to work for some. For the rest of us, there's sports.

> *Sometimes you eat the bear, and sometimes the bear eats you.*

The nice thing about sports is that you have a reasonable chance of survival. The violence is artificially contained by rules. While there is the challenge of risk and the threat of bodily harm, at least there's a structure to the madness. Sports provide a great way to burn off the frustration that accrues with life on planet Earth.

If nothing else, sports are an escape from the noise and uncertainty of everyday life. Eisenhower played golf just to get away from the pressures of the presidency. It did him good to concentrate on a whole new set of problems.

Sports are decisive. There's a winner and a loser. Sometimes you eat the bear, and sometimes the bear eats you. A lot of the rest of life is pretty indecisive. It can seem like a never-ending sitcom—or worse—the feeling you get after two hours and twenty minutes of *The English Patient*. Will the subplots *ever* be resolved?

Prove Your Merit

Proving merit is about courage—courage in the face of adversity and risk. It's about physical prowess and often the ability to play through

34 PROVE YOUR MERIT

Proving merit is about courage—courage in the face of adversity and risk. It's about physical prowess and often the ability to play through pain and the fear of injury. Earning the peak experience is what it's all about. The arena gives us the chance to get there, to experience that feeling of invincibility, when no one can stop you.

some pain and the fear of injury. Go back and watch Isiah Thomas in the 1988 NBA Finals. He scored 45 points with a sprained ankle. He got 25 in the fourth quarter, and he could hardly walk.

Kobe Bryant did the same thing with his bad ankle in the overtime of Game 4 of the 2000 Finals. When Shaq fouled out in overtime, Kobe just took over. He became Michael Jordan.

Having screwed up my ankles a few times, I find that somewhat inspirational. I know what it's like to feel that kind of pain and to wonder if it's going to hurt more if I screw it up again.

Sports are inspirational. That's a good thing. Earning the peak experience is what it's all about. The arena gives us the chance to get there—to experience that feeling of invincibility, when no one can stop you.

Of course there are valleys. But it's worth going through them to get to the peak. It keeps us coming back.

The Battle of Good and Evil

With each sport comes a structure. With each structure comes an ethic. Into the ethic come the players, the personalities, and the teams. And good and evil. It's always in there somewhere.

The job of the hero is to find the evil and root it out.

Why do we root for one team and not another? Because we see the good in one and the downside of the other. We're finding good; we're finding evil. We do this within a structure. We relate to teammates in a certain way, and so there is teamwork. We relate to opponents in another way, and that is sportsmanship. Although we think of them as the enemy, we act toward them within the rules. That's sportsmanship. For a while we don't like them. They're the bad guys. It's not war, but it's not Sunday school either.

We're supposed to find the good in people?

We're simulating the epic battles of life. Ugly, ugly, battles.

During the game it's just the opposite. Find the evil. Destroy it. Find the good after the game. We're simulating the epic battles of life. Ugly, ugly battles. Think of them that way. It's an arena.

Understand the System

Nobody's giving sportsmanship awards. If they are, nobody seems to care. I didn't make it that way, I'm simply commenting. Who was the NBA sportsman of the year? Baseball? Football? It's a sad commentary, but it's true.

Society rewards the achiever and ignores character. That's the system you're in. It doesn't mean you shouldn't develop character. You should. Just don't expect to be rewarded for it on this Earth. You need to achieve.

Understand what you're getting into. Sports are not pretty. Remember the Roman arena. And put on the full armor. You're going to need it.

TRAIN TOUGH CHALLENGE

- The arena can be an ugly place. You don't have to be ugly.

- Have something to prove. Prove your merit.

- For a while we won't like our opponents. That's OK.

- You need to achieve. That's the way the world works.

14

LEARN FROM THE GREAT ONES

★

Nothing arouses ambition so much as the trumpet clang of another's fame.

—BALTASAR GRACIAN

Go ahead, have some heroes. Identify with them; be a bit of a fan. Get yourself inspired. Dream.

Being a fan is a way to relate, especially for guys. What else are we going to talk about?

You learn a lot following a team or a player. You put yourself in their shoes; you get a feel for what they're going through. Every once in a while you get surprised, and you have to ask the all-important question: "How'd they do that?"

Loser Mentality: They lucked out.
Train Tough Attitude: I've got to figure out how they did that.

Dynasties

It takes a unique set of circumstances for a team to dominate over a number of years. It takes extraordinary players, superb coaching, dedication, and a sustainable reason for confidence. You need to know what it takes for a team to dominate over a period of years. Here are three for all time:

The Bill Russell Boston Celtics

Bill Russell won the NCAA Championship twice with the University of San Francisco. He postponed his professional debut to play for the 1956 U.S. gold medal Olympic team. In his first 10 years in the NBA, his Celtics won the championship nine times, losing only when Russell was out with an injury.

He won the NBA Most Valuable Player Award five times. He became the Celtics' player-coach in 1966 and guided them to two more championships in 1968 and 1969. His matchups against Wilt Chamberlain were the most impressive—the only time he played as an underdog. He always found a way to stymie Wilt. In all, the Russell Celtics won the championship 11 out of his 13 years.

Always a perfectionist, Russell graded his performances on a 100-point scale. He never scored himself above a 65.

The Vince Lombardi Green Bay Packers

Vince Lombardi took over the Green Bay Packers in 1959, after they had won only one game the year before. They went 7–5 in his first year and went to the Western Division title game the following year, losing the only postseason game Lombardi would ever lose. During the next seven years, the Packers finished at the top of the pro football heap five times—an incredible accomplishment.

Lombardi believed football was "a game for madmen," that it was "hit or be hit," and that the game was by definition "a cruel business." He used fear to motivate his players, keeping them off balance, never comfortable. His message was a mixture of love and hate—hate to stoke the fire of competitiveness and love to help a teammate who wasn't perfect.

He instilled confidence and pride in his players, rewarding individual excellence in weekly award ceremonies. Lombardi expected talent to be used to its fullest in supporting the team and 100 percent effort at all times. He was a master of motivation, collecting motivational sayings, which he used in speeches and posted on the locker room walls.

"There are other coaches who know more about Xs and Os," he said, "but I have an edge. I know more about football players than they do."

The John Wooden UCLA Bruins

What John Wooden accomplished at UCLA will never be duplicated. His teams won seven consecutive NCAA Basketball Championships, had four seasons in which they won all 30 games, won 38 consecutive games in NCAA tournament play, and had an 88-game winning streak. The Bruins won the NCAA Championship 10 times in 12 years.

Wooden was a church deacon who didn't smoke, drink, or use profanity. He appeared amazingly calm and collected no matter what the game situation.

It was during practice that he drove his team, insisting on 100 percent concentration and effort. A fast-break proponent, Wooden told his team that 50 percent of their wins would be earned in the last five minutes of the game—when their superior conditioning would pay off.

Wooden liked to keep things simple, insisting that his players follow a basic eating, resting, and game-day routine. He watched the little things, even instructing players on how to wear their socks.

He realized the team couldn't win every game, though they often seemed to. Sometimes the other team would just be better that night, he told his team, just don't beat yourself. A basic tenet of his offensive strategy was equally simple: get the ball to the guy who's hot.

---

35 DOMINATE

It takes a unique set of circumstances for a team to dominate over a season or a number of years. It takes extraordinary players with a team orientation, superb coaching, dedication, and a sustainable reason for confidence.

Underdogs

I love underdogs. If I'm watching a game I don't know much about, all I have to do is find out who's supposed to lose, and I wind up pulling for them. There's nothing better than an upset. There's nothing better for focus than being told you're not supposed to win. We saw it in the 2001 World Series with the Arizona Diamondbacks upsetting the New York Yankees and again in Super Bowl XXXVI with the New England Patriots upsetting the St. Louis Rams. Those were good ones, but I want to take you back in the day. Here are my four all-time favorite upsets. See what you can learn.

The World Champion Cleveland Browns

The date was December 27, 1964, and I, along with 79,553 other fans, sat in subfreezing temperature in a 20-mile-an-hour wind in Cleveland's Municipal Stadium. I had turned 13 the day before, and I was due for one more birthday present. The underdog Browns were playing host to the highly touted Baltimore Colts for the NFL Championship. Depending on whose point spread you believed, the Browns were anywhere from 7- to 20-point underdogs to the 12–2 Colts.

The Colts had crushed the Browns in their previous two meetings. Johnny Unitas and Don Shula of the Colts were Player and Coach of the Year, respectively. *Sports Illustrated* already planned to feature the two of them on a cover—immediately after they won the championship. The Colts' superior offense was supposed to dominate the highly suspect Browns defense.

But the Browns did their homework. Blanton Collier, the Browns coach and a film junkie, kept finding new ways he thought his defense could pressure the Colts. Much of what he saw were little things, ways his linemen could out-technique their opponents and bring pressure to bear on Unitas.

Bernie Parrish, a Browns cornerback, wondered aloud why other teams gave Colts receivers Raymond Berry and Jimmy Orr so much room off the line of scrimmage. Most of the Colts passes were timing patterns that might be upset by contact at the line of scrimmage. The Browns decided they would smother the Colts receivers, keeping them off their routes.

By the end of the two-week preparation period, the Browns were convinced they could win. I was privileged to be around a number of players the morning of the game. One of my early mentors was Bill Glass, a primary pass rusher for the Browns. He and his teammates exuded a quiet confidence that belied the predictions.

And well they should have. The game plan worked to perfection, and the Browns triumphed, 27–0.

Those guys were ready!

Muhammad Ali Versus George Foreman

Every athlete should study the career of Muhammad Ali. You should watch the tapes, looking to understand the prefight strategy and the round-by-round adjustments.

There was no one like Muhammad Ali. Initially despised for his braggadocio, he came to be loved by the entire world. He had epic battles with Ken Norton and Joe Frazier. He tamed Sonny Liston when Liston was believed to be unbeatable. But my personal favorite was the "rumble in the jungle," fought against George Foreman in Zaire on October 30, 1974.

The issue was not whether Ali would win the fight but whether he would survive it. Foreman's record was 40–0, with 37 knockouts. No fight in his previous eight had gone beyond the second round, including fights with Ken Norton and Joe Frazier, both of whom had beaten the aging Ali. Foreman had made mincemeat of Frazier. "My opponents don't worry about losing," Foreman said, "they worry about getting hurt."

This was not the friendly George Foreman we've since come to know and love. This was the mean, surly Foreman of his early days. He was like nothing the boxing world had ever seen.

Ali alone remained supremely confident, nicknaming Foreman "the Mummy" and insisting that George would have nothing to hit.

Incredibly, Ali adjusted his fight strategy on the fly. Thirty seconds into round two, he retreated to the ropes, testing what he would later call his "rope-a-dope" technique. He blocked some shots with his arms, leaned away from others, and absorbed a growing number of vicious blows. It was frightening to behold. Ali's corner screamed for him to dance. For a while it looked like he was tanking the fight.

In the fifth round the end seemed near, but Ali hung on to finish strong. He survived rounds six and seven, and at that point it was Foreman who looked tired. At the start of the eighth, Ali told Foreman, "Now it's my turn."

Ali had taken Foreman's best shot, what Foreman called "the hardest shot to the body I had ever delivered to any opponent." Noticing Ali had cringed, Foreman thought his moment had come. "And then he looked at me," recalled Foreman. "He had that look in his eyes, like he was saying, 'I'm not gonna let you hurt me.'"

Punched out, Foreman chased Ali with his hands down. Foreman missed with a right that threw him off balance. Ali countered with a huge right that sent Foreman spinning out of control toward the canvas. Ali was bouncing, wondering whether to unload again as George headed down. It was a moment of high art. Ali restrained himself, his work finished. Foreman stayed down.

The 1980 U.S. Olympic Hockey Team

It helped to be in the United States military to fully appreciate how low morale was early in 1980. American hostages were being held in Iran; the Soviet invasion of Afghanistan cast a pall over the games. President Jimmy Carter hinted that the country seemed to be suffering through a malaise.

Help came from an unexpected quarter—the United States Olympic hockey team. Early on, Coach Herb Brooks developed a strategy that took advantage of the one-hundred-foot-wide Olympic rink, using a soccer-style offense that depended on long, accurate passes. It was the same system the Soviets used to embarrass the NHL in international competition. But there was one difference—Brooks wanted to keep the North American tradition of close, hard body checking, especially in front of the net, which he dubbed "bloody nose alley."

Despite hard training and a rigorous exhibition season, the Americans hardly seemed ready for the competition. Pundits figured they'd do well to place fifth or sixth. Three days before the start of the Olympics they lost to the Soviets, 10–3, in Madison Square Garden. The Soviet system had won the previous four Olympic gold medals and 16 amateur world championships. The six months the U.S. team spent training together couldn't compare to the Soviets, many of whom had played together for 10 years. The average age of the U.S. team was 21.

But something special was happening at Lake Placid. In their first game, against Sweden, the U.S. team trailed the entire game before tying it with just 27 seconds remaining. Then they upset a veteran Czechoslovakian team, 7–3. Then Norway fell, then Romania. Then it was a come-from-behind 4–2 win over West Germany. Suddenly the nation took notice—next up was the powerful Soviet team.

The Americans trailed throughout the first period before tying the score, 2–2, with a last-second goal. The Soviets answered early in the second, to go up, 3–2. But goalie Jim Craig would not let them score again, stopping shot after shot from the frustrated Soviets. The Americans ended the second period just one goal down.

The Soviets seemed to tire in the third. The United States scored at 8:39 and scored again a minute and a half later. The Olympic field house shook with chants of "USA, USA!" America held its breath as the team hung on to win. It may well have been the most significant documented upset in the history of sports.

Two nights later the team came from behind to beat Finland, 4–2, and garner the gold. A team with any less character could easily have succumbed to a postgame letdown against a tough Finnish team. They did us proud.

Rulon Gardner Defeats Alexander Karelin in the 2000 Olympics

Wrestler Alexander Karelin was a Russian legend. He hadn't lost a Greco-Roman match in 13 years, garnering three Olympic golds and seven World Championships. He hadn't been scored on in 10 years. Matt Ghaffari, one of America's best heavyweights, pursued Karelin for years. His record against the Russian: a perfect 0–23.

At six feet, four inches, and 290 pounds, Karelin was an imposing figure with his Mr. Clean bald head and muscular body. He grew up hauling logs across the frozen tundra of Siberia, rowing alone on the lakes in spring. He once lugged a refrigerator up seven flights of stairs. Except for having earned the accolade of "the Greatest Wrestler Who Ever Lived," Karelin's country background was not so different from that of Rulon Gardner, who grew up half a world away.

Gardner was a farm boy, who worked bailing hay and slinging manure in the rarified air of Afton, Wyoming, which his mother described as, "somewhere near Idaho." Dubbed "Fatso" by his schoolmates, Gardner had a rounded physique and bemused demeanor that contrasted with his Russian opponent.

So did his record.

Gardner's claim to fame was a fourth-place finish in the 1993 NCAAs while a student at the University of Nebraska. He placed fifth in world competition in 1997, losing to Karelin, 5–0, noting that when he pushed against Karelin, "it was like pushing against a horse." Gardner had never won a medal in international competition.

Still, Gardner exuded a quiet confidence in the hours leading up to his match with Karelin. His entire family—he was the youngest of nine children—was on hand in Sydney to see the match. Like most heavyweight wrestling matches, it was largely a series of pushes and shoves, except that in the second period, Karelin made a mistake. His hands separated during a clinch with the rotund Gardner, and Gardner was awarded a point.

36 BEAT THE ODDS

What does it take for an underdog to win? Preparation. Determination.
Leadership. Surprise.

Through the rest of the match Gardner refused to yield, effectively
warding off the best the Russian had to offer. By the end, Karelin was
gasping for air, helplessly mumbling, "I give up" as the clock wound
down to end the match, sealing perhaps the biggest upset in Olympic
wrestling history.

"He wrestled the perfect match," said U.S. Greco-Roman coach
Steve Fraser. "Absolutely perfect."

And what were the ingredients in Gardner's success?

Fraser cited Gardner's conditioning and will.

"Nobody ever wants to wrestle Gardner in practice," said Coach
Fraser, "because he never lets up."

Under Pressure

Don't you just love to watch athletes under pressure—wondering how
they're going to respond, watching for those telltale signs to see how
they're handling it? How do you respond to pressure? Because one
of our goals is to make you "automatic" when the heat's on, read the
following three examples, and know that it can be done.

Doug Collins at the Free Throw Line

The United States of America had never lost an Olympic basketball
game—a record spanning 62 victories. Yet in the gold medal final of
the 1972 Munich Olympics, they trailed the powerful Soviet team
from the opening tip.

With six seconds remaining and the United States still trailing,
49–48, a young U.S. player named Doug Collins stole the ball. Doug

would go on to a successful professional career as a player, coach, and commentator.

Doug was fouled with three seconds on the clock.

He sank the game-tying free throw.

The time-out horn unexpectedly sounded as he released the second. It didn't matter—Doug sank it anyway.

The Soviets quickly inbounded the ball, but two seconds later the referee stopped play, awarding the Soviets a time-out. In what remains the most notorious ending in basketball history, they were given a reset to three seconds and scored the winning basket.

The Americans were stunned, and they later refused to accept their silver medals. Ironically, U.S. coach Hank Iba had his pocket picked while filing the official protest.

The United States' run ingloriously ended, and Doug Collins's sinking of the two biggest free throws in U.S. history became but a footnote. Still, you can't take away the kind of courage it took to knock those babies down.

Mary Lou Retton Nails the Vault

At four feet, nine inches, and 109 pounds, Mary Lou Retton hardly had the ideal body for a gymnast. Worse, she underwent knee surgery two months before the 1984 Olympic games in Los Angeles. Up to that time, no American woman had ever won an individual Olympic medal in gymnastics. Capitalizing on her extraordinarily muscular frame to catapult her through explosive movements, Mary Lou would win four.

In the final round of the all-around competition, Retton was 0.05 points behind Ecaterina Szabo of Romania. Szabo went first on the uneven bars, scoring a brilliant 9.9 and putting unbelievable pressure on Mary Lou for a perfect score on the vault.

Tapes capture her coach frantically insisting, "You can do it," as Mary Lou looks with the eye of the tiger. Perhaps at 16 years of age she had not yet learned fear. If she had, she didn't show it.

The arena fell silent as she sprinted down the runway, hit the springboard, and twisted perfectly in midair. The roar of the crowd told the world it had just witnessed perfection.

In the words of one pundit, "Mary Lou Retton took the 1984 Olympics and turned them into a song."

Mookie Wilson at the Plate

Baseball fans everywhere remember the ball going through Bill Buckner's legs in Game 6 of the '86 Series, but does anybody remember who hit it?

I attended Games 1 and 2 of the Series at Shea Stadium, games the Red Sox won. I was in both clubhouses after Game 2. Let me tell you what I saw. The Mets were cool as cucumbers, saying all the right things and seemingly unconcerned about losing the first two games at home. The Red Sox were euphoric, almost immature. I figured that somehow, the Mets were going to be all right.

Mookie Wilson hit the dribbler that won Game 6 in Boston. He did it on the 10th pitch—after hitting foul after foul with two strikes off an overpowering Bob Stanley. There has never been a more determined at-bat in the history of baseball. Mookie simply refused to go down, so the Red Sox had to go instead—and they were just one strike away from winning their first World Series since 1918.

Magic Moments

There are some moments in sports that just make you stop and say, "Wow, that's really what it's all about." We're talking inspiration here, Baby, and we can always use a little of that. Try these three for size:

Pete Rose Is There for the Catch

Pete Rose had a 24-year major league playing career during which time he won three batting titles, won an MVP Award, and broke Ty Cobb's career hit record. He probably had average talent, but he parlayed what he had into the record books. Known throughout his career as "Charlie Hustle," Rose worked and played harder than any man ever to play the game. He ran to first base, even on walks.

But it was a defensive play that captured the essence of Pete Rose. It came late in his career, while he played first base for the Philadelphia Phillies in Game 6 of the 1980 World Series. With the Phils up 4–1, the Kansas City Royals had the bases loaded and one out in the top of the ninth.

Frank White popped up near the Phils' dugout, and catcher Bob Boone called for the ball. At the last second he seemed to lose it and the ball popped out of his glove. Rose, hovering nearby and ready for anything, neatly snagged the carom for the out. One strikeout later, the Phillies were world champions.

Most infielders would have missed the opportunity. Hey, the other guy called it. Not Rose—he epitomized readiness on a ballfield.

Michael Jordan Hits the Jumper

It was Game 6 of the 1998 NBA Finals, and the Utah Jazz were in position to knot the series—the Chicago Bulls had a chance to win it outright. The Jazz led most of the way, but the Bulls kept hanging around.

When John Stockton hit a three-pointer with 41.9 seconds remaining in the game, the Utah Jazz moved ahead, 86–83. The Salt Palace was bedlam. It may be the loudest arena in the world. The Bulls looked tired.

Tex Winter, the Bulls' assistant coach, drew up a play for Jordan during the ensuing time-out. Jordan took Byron Russell one-on-one to the right side, driving all the way to the basket, laying it high off the glass and in. The Bulls trailed, 86–85, with 37 seconds remaining.

37 HAVE SOME HEROES

Go ahead, have some heroes. Identify with them; be a bit of a fan. Get yourself inspired. Realizing they're human, study their magic moments, how they performed as underdogs, how they performed under pressure, and how they built dynasties. Don't fall for the fallacy that heroes have it made. Remember something else: the obstacles they had to overcome.

Stockton casually brought the ball downcourt as the clock wound down. He passed to Karl Malone with 11 seconds left on the shot clock and 26 seconds left in the game. Jordan sneaked in behind Malone, delicately extending himself, and stole the ball. There were 18 seconds left as Jordan started upcourt with the ball, the Bulls out of time-outs. The crowd grew strangely quiet at the ominous turn of events.

Utah had Byron Russell alone on Jordan. At eight seconds, Russell made a wild swipe at the ball. Jordan deftly avoided the attack and made a move of his own toward the basket. Russell, already having been burned in that direction, overreacted to cut Jordan off. It was too late. In perfect control, Jordan squared up to shoot, leaving Russell sprawling to recover.

He buried the shot—what was thought to be his final shot in the NBA—and the Bulls had their sixth championship of the Jordan era.

Tara Lapinski Wins the Gold

For the sheer thrill of victory, you have to go back only to Tara Lapinski watching the final scores go up at the 1998 Winter Olympics in Nagano, Japan. She and Michelle Kwan both skated brilliantly, but Lapinski clearly took more chances—and they paid off.

Tara's reaction to winning the gold is the ecstasy we all dream about—it's Christmas, winning the lottery, and Grandma coming back from the dead all rolled up into one. It was a happiness she earned through hard work and a gutsy performance. The emotion was expressed so purely it could come only from a 14-year-old.

They should take that tape and show it to depressed people. Just watching someone that happy has to rub off. It sure works for me.

Heroes Aren't Born, They're Made

Go ahead—have some heroes. Realizing they're human, study their magic moments, how they perform as underdogs or under pressure, how they built dynasties. Remember something else: the obstacles they had to overcome. Don't fall for the fallacy that heroes have it made. Consider this:

Michael Jordan was cut from his high school basketball team as a sophomore. His friend, Leroy Smith, another sophomore, made the team. Jordan spent the afternoon crying in his room, and then he resolved to make himself a better player. Years later, as a Chicago Bull, he would check into hotel rooms using the alias Leroy Smith.

Bill Russell also failed to make his varsity high school team as a sophomore. He was third string as a junior and didn't start until his senior year.

Jim Brown, a member of the 1964 Cleveland Browns championship team and arguably the greatest running back ever to play the game, was fifth string as a sophomore at Syracuse University. He was told he would never be a running back, that he belonged on the line. Brown didn't start until there were three games left in the season, and then only because two other backs were injured. He gained 151 yards that day, and the rest is history.

These are just some things you might want to keep in mind when things aren't going your way. You become a hero by overcoming obstacles; without obstacles, there are no heroes.

TRAIN TOUGH CHALLENGE

- Identify your sports heroes. What qualities can you learn from them?

- Remember, heroes aren't born, they're made. Without adversity, there are no heroes.

15

SEX, DRUGS, AND ROCK 'N' ROLL

★

If you make the right decisions when faced with ethical problems, you will continually build your character and your leadership.
—ARMY FIELD MANUAL 22-100, *MILITARY LEADERSHIP*

OK, it's time for me to put on my pleasure policeman's hat and pull you over to the side of the road. Time to remind you of all the rules your buddies told you were made to be broken.

First of all, here's the good news. You can break all of the rules we'll talk about and still be a star—if you're good enough. It's been done. It's done all the time. Sure, we see a few guys hit the wall, but for every one of them there are many who get by.

It's kind of like driving. You can cruise with a taillight out, speed, litter, and do a half a dozen other stupid things, and the odds are you won't get caught or have an accident. On any given day, the odds are in your favor.

A new driver is amazed at the freedom he feels driving a car. Then he starts testing the rules. Pretty soon it's: "Hey, I can speed. Nothing happens." Then it's: "Gee, I was pretty drunk last night and I still made it home." But he's not looking at the big picture. He doesn't realize that the odds are one in three that he'll be in a serious-injury accident in his lifetime and that he can cut those odds in half or double them just by the way he drives.

A good athlete isn't necessarily going to be destroyed because he drinks, does drugs, and gambles. These are things a gifted athlete can sometimes carry.

In the Army we call it putting rocks in the rucksack. A rucksack is a big, canvas bag in which a soldier carries his gear. He's got X amount of gear to haul and Y amount of space to put it in. There's always room for a few rocks. Some soldiers like to see if they can still carry the bag with some extra stuff in it. A couple of rocks are no big deal—until you carry the bag for a while. Then they become a real burden. Why would anyone want to carry rocks?

Regardless of who you are, the lighter the bag, the farther you go.

Loser Mentality: I can party tonight and play tomorrow.
Train Tough Attitude: No thanks. I've got a game this week.

Alcohol

Alcohol is a socially acceptable way to get high. Initially at least, alcohol produces feelings of increased self-worth and seems to increase our ability to relate and communicate.

Drink responsibly, cut back if necessary, or abstain altogether.

For many, the buzz of alcohol isn't worth the headache they have the next day. One-third of Americans never touch the stuff.

Some people drink without problems. Other folks are prone to have problems with drinking and should steer clear.

Is there a personality profile for the problem drinker?

People drink for many reasons, but those who get frustrated easily, have low self-worth, and who feel isolated or "different" are most at risk. The ability to "hold your liquor" is one of several indicators that alcohol might be a larger problem for you than for most people, as is a family history of alcoholism.

Let's face it: alcohol causes a lot of problems. First of all, 20 percent of the people are consuming 80 percent of the alcohol. Broken down further, 7 percent of the population do 50 percent of the drinking. You have your dependent crowd who can't quit and your alcohol abusers who drink and drive and cause a whole host of other problems. Heavy drinkers decrease their ability for abstract thought and problem solving and lose physical dexterity and visual skills—and that's when they're tested sober.

The list of alcohol-related illnesses is too long to go into. Suffice it to say you can pretty much kill yourself with a fifth of 100-proof liquor or by "chug-a-lugging" 10 to 16 beers. It's a hell of a way to go.

If you're watching your weight, you better be watching what you drink. Alcohol adds seven empty calories per gram and provides absolutely zero nutritional value. In fact, it actually interferes with the body's ability to absorb nutrients. It also slows by a third the rate at which the body burns fat. So not only are you adding worthless calories, you're burning them more slowly.

College administrators estimate that about a third of all academic problems are alcohol related and that alcohol is directly responsible for a quarter of all dropouts. Yet about a third of the revenue for college newspapers comes from alcohol ads. Like I say, it's socially acceptable.

It's a big rock in the rucksack. Drink responsibly, cut back if necessary, or abstain altogether. Get help if you need it.

Gambling

I never had much problem with gambling because I hate to lose. Chronic casino gamblers describe themselves as "happy" if they can stretch a set amount of money for four hours instead of two. That was never my idea of happiness.

Many athletes are expressly forbidden from betting on games in the sport in which they play. This prohibition is designed to protect the integrity of sports. But the limitations on gambling are growing fewer and fewer as Americans wager more and more money in an ever-expanding variety of venues. The latest lines and point spreads are available in many sports sections.

> *Gambling is a counterproductive activity for athletes.*

In a sense, athletes are gamblers in that we bet on ourselves and our ability to persevere. We do the work and then depend on ourselves and our teammates to carry the day. Feeling good about winning and learning from losing is enough for us. Not only have we increased our physical fitness, but we carry away a certain satisfaction in having played the game.

Gamblers like to think of themselves as athletes, involved in a quest. They report a "rush" very much like the one the athlete feels at the moment of truth in sports. Gamblers try to beat the dealer, beat the machine, or beat the spread. There's a whole psychology to how they operate, including keeping a positive attitude. It's really kind of pathetic.

Gambling is a counterproductive activity for athletes. While we're screwing around with point spreads or sitting in front of a video game, we're also wasting valuable competitive energy. Bet on yourself, without wagering money. You're already wagering your name and reputation every time you suit up. Isn't that enough?

Sex

Nobody wants to talk about how many athletes have had their numbers go down behind a screwed-up sex life. It's pretty tough to keep stats on this one. This one's a little more personal. But it's still important.

The question you need to ask yourself is simply: "Is my sex life in any way hindering my performance?" Give yourself an honest answer. Then come up with a plan to do something about it.

An athlete in an unhappy relationship carries the problem with him. A guy in two or more unhappy relationships just compounds the problem. A guy who can't take his eyes off the cheerleaders is distracted. A guy who chases and carries on gets worn out.

Let's face it: love is the toughest game in town. It's got it's own bumps and bruises, and no matter who you are, love games are going to be a distraction. If you're a player and this is your game, fine, but don't expect to be the same athlete on the field. You won't be.

> *Love is the toughest game in town.*

Rock 'n' Roll

Rock 'n' roll. Rap. Disco. Grunge. The party train. Music has the power to transform our mood and our thinking. Most of the time that's a good thing. A world without music would be a world without song. The closest we could get then would be poetry—that would be pretty tough.

I grew up with Led Zeppelin, the Stones, Janis Joplin, and the Jimi Hendrix Experience. In the Army my black friends turned me on to the Gap Band, Morris Day, and that guy sometimes known as Prince. I can turn my baseball cap around and hip-hop with the best of them.

There's a time and a place.

Make sure you know the time and place. It's probably not on the way to the game. In college my buddy and I used to crank up his car stereo on the way to baseball games. We rocked. We got all pumped up on those two-hour trips—and then had nothing left for the game. We left it all in his car.

★ 38 SAVE THE PARTY

Some athletes put as much emphasis on their social life as they do on their sport. Some of them get away with it. But would they be more effective if they had themselves more under control? The answer is "yes!" Every time. Save the party for after you've won the championship.

The best time to take a ride on the party train is when there's no game or practice the next day—because you just won the championship.

Tobacco

Cigarettes kill more Americans each year than AIDS, alcohol, car accidents, murders, suicides, drugs, and fires combined. Eighty-five percent of men with lung cancer and 75 percent of women with lung cancer smoke.

Cigar smokers are less likely than cigarette smokers to get lung cancer. But they're more likely than nonsmokers to get cancers of the larynx, mouth, and esophagus—as well as lung cancer.

Very few serious athletes smoke. It's almost a contradiction in terms. Most of us have seen smokers try to run and then complain of shortness of breath. Those that quit find that their lung function increases up to 30 percent after a couple of months. My heart goes out to those who struggle with this problem. The easiest way to stay on top of it is to never start in the first place.

Smokeless tobacco provides an even better rush as more nicotine reaches the bloodstream. While the dangers of lung cancer for smokeless users are less than for smokers, smokeless users risk an array of dental problems and increased risk of oral, pharynx, and esophageal cancers. The image of the macho rodeo rider or ballplayer with a chew has tarnished. Thanks go out to Brett Butler, a former user, for speaking out against this scourge after his throat surgery.

Given what we know about tobacco use, it's still not hard to understand why people start. It's called advertising—that and the free endorsement these products receive every time a Hollywood movie shows a star lighting up. These people will whine all year to save the whale, but they don't seem to care about the health habits of human beings.

Makes you kind of glad to be an athlete, doesn't it?

Painkillers

Pain exists to warn us that a body part is damaged and should be rested, repaired, or protected. It's a frequent by-product of athletic endeavor. Many of us use aspirin, acetaminophen, naproxen sodium, or ibuprofen to combat minor aches and pains that crop up along the way. Sometimes doctors will prescribe more powerful painkillers.

Muscle relaxants can be used to treat strains, sprains, and spasms. Some athletes make the mistake of using muscle relaxants to combat performance anxiety, a not-so-smart idea as these drugs also cause sedation, depression, blurred vision, decreased concentration, and mild euphoria. I once played golf using a muscle relaxant for my back. I think I had all the symptoms except euphoria; it was a miserable round.

Antiinflammatory drugs lessen pain and decrease swelling—they are not a cure. They can help an athlete return to activity after an injury but should be part of a careful analysis of associated risks.

As an athlete, you are expected to play through pain. Part of proving yourself is minimizing the effect of pain and injury. There's nothing more disgusting than watching a player dramatize his injury or quit because he's in a bit of pain.

Football players especially have to play through pain. If a football player waits until everything feels right, the season will be long over. Football players are always banged up—and there's always another guy waiting in the wings for open positions if you can't hack it. Nobody wants the "injury-prone" tag.

With this kind of pressure, it's no wonder there are problems. Trainers, coaches, players, and physicians all struggle to find the right mix of when a player should play, rest, or play under medication. The story of quarterback Brett Favre's 1995 season is a case study on the dangers of overusing painkillers.

> *If a football player waits until everything feels right, the season will be long over.*

Favre, known as a tough ugly for his ability to play with pain, had already undergone numerous surgeries prior to the '95 season. By midseason he had turf toe, a bruised shoulder on his throwing arm, an arthritic hip, a bruised knee, and a bad back. Yet with painkillers, he was still able to perform. Favre was taking Vicodin, a narcotic-analgesic painkiller, and he was grubbing extra pills from his teammates. Combined with his considerable alcohol intake throughout the season, it made for a dangerous ride. It was only after the season, when Favre had a life-threatening seizure, that he was forced to deal with what had become an addiction to the Vicodin.

Favre had hidden his addiction well but, by his own admission, paid a tremendous price psychologically, as he struggled to ride out an emotional roller coaster. It took a lot of courage and professional help for Brett Favre to get back on track. Yet his story is not that unusual in a game that causes a lot of pain and rewards those who play through that pain.

Forewarned is forearmed.

Steroids and Performance-Enhancing Drugs

The drive to excel causes many athletes to cross the line. Ask athletes if they would take a drug that would take them to the top of their sport but kill them within the year, and most of them say yes. Then look at China's infantile quest to prove themselves to the world and how they have systematically used steroids to try and take over women's swimming and weightlifting. It's a big problem. Do we want to reward hard work and courage, or science?

There's no question that anabolic-androgenic steroids are being widely abused worldwide. These drugs produce incredible results in terms of body weight, lean muscle mass, and strength. Derived from male testosterone or synthesized versions of it, they also increase aggressiveness and confidence—both useful traits in sports. Young athletes use steroids to mature sooner or to look like their friends who are already using.

There is a serious downside to steroid use. The young athlete who uses may mature and develop sooner, but steroids also stunt growth, limiting increases in height. Users are known by a bloated appearance. Extended use results in a long-term decrease in the body's natural ability to produce testosterone. Worse, steroid use results in bone weakness, tendon injuries, cancer, and sexual problems. Steroids masculinize women and, strangely, tend to feminize men, decreasing sex organ size and swelling breasts. Heavy users are more irritable and more prone to violence, and they sometimes experience psychotic symptoms with grandiose illusions or paranoia. Withdrawal symptoms include fatigue, depression, restlessness, insomnia, loss of appetite, and diminished sexual desire.

You would think the obvious downside to steroids would discourage use, but it doesn't. The only way we're going to get a level playing field is through extensive, comprehensive testing. It's a shame the honest athlete has to have his privacy invaded to ensure his sport is clean, but that's a price we must pay. Because there are countries that will systematically abuse these substances, we must have tough, tested policies if international competition is going to mean anything. You abuse, you lose.

Let's let the athletes compete on the field and have the scientists compete somewhere else.

I submitted to random urinalysis for 20 years in the Army, and I got used to it. It was worth it to deter drug use and keep the team clean in a life-and-death industry. There's no place in sports for performance-enhancing drugs that alter fair competition—and that includes beta-blockers, diuretics, and blood doping.

Let's let the athletes compete on the field and have the scientists compete somewhere else. Speaking of which, what happened to our plans to colonize the moon?

Street Drugs

Athletes are adventurous by nature and learn to live with a certain amount of risk. Using street drugs provides plenty of both adventure

---

39 JUST SAY "NO"

When it comes to gambling, drunkenness, illegal drug use, steroids, and tobacco the answer is obvious. Keep it real simple on this one. Just say "no."

and risk. You never really know what you're taking and what it's been cut with. You get a temporary escape, maybe even a permanent one.

Using street drugs is usually a social thing, so you wind up running with a certain set of people and copping their attitude. Is this something that's going to improve your game? How would getting busted affect your career?

I'm not going to give a laundry list of the effects of the street drugs that are out there. Fortunately, there's now plenty of information available, and kids are getting it at an early age in school. You either buy in to the notion that illegal drugs are an unnecessary danger or you don't. You live with the consequences of your choices. Just saying "no" is too simple for some people.

Ultimately you decide how and what to think about this issue . . . and whether to add another rock to your rucksack.

It's always going to be your call.

Have a nice day.

TRAIN TOUGH CHALLENGE

How about we take some rocks out of the rucksack instead of putting them in?

Just say "no"—how hard is that?

16

NOT FOR MEN ONLY

★

We are not interested in the possibilities of defeat.
— QUEEN VICTORIA

I've always loved this quote from Queen Victoria. Imagine a couple of diplomats coming in to brief Her Majesty and getting midway through their introduction when she interrupts with that announcement. "How's about we focus on winning, fellas," she seems to be saying.

Of course there are some situations where you just can't win. The evolving role of women in society is one of them. Everyone has an opinion, nobody agrees on everything, and it's easy to get emotional.

We live in a society that changes at warp speed, with the rate of change accelerating. That makes for a certain amount of discomfort between the sexes. Are you feeling it? I know I am.

Typical Jock Mentality: I hate change.
Train Tough Attitude: The only thing constant is change.

Women Need Sports, Too

Playing sports has proved to be a great way for women—like men—to keep fit, improve their physical and mental skills, and develop confidence. The lessons learned on the playing field are just as valuable for women as they are for men.

The confidence women build on the athletic field carries over to careers. Of women business leaders in major companies, 80 percent say they were tomboys who were involved in sports.

The arena's a tough place for women; it's hardly a level playing field.

Young women who exercise are 92 percent less likely to use drugs, 80 percent less likely to have an unwanted pregnancy, and three times more likely to graduate from high school. Young women who don't exercise experience greater instances of depression, exhaustion, chronic illness, and suicide.

Women who exercise during menopause have fewer problems with hot flashes, fatigue, depression, irritability, and weight gain. Later in life they fare better against osteoporosis and arteriosclerosis.

With the advent of Title IX in 1972, women were guaranteed equal opportunity in education and athletics. Amazingly, it's 30 years later and only 10 percent of schools and colleges are in compliance. It'll supposedly take another 10 years to bring them into line.

Some prejudices die hard, and women are up against it from early childhood when they're dressed all in pink and told to play nicely. While we encourage athleticism in boys, we largely ignore it in our girls. Boys are taught to throw; girls aren't. Then we point out that girls throw funny.

According to one study, girls are less likely to be called on by a teacher in class and are less likely to speak up in class. While boys are praised for academic work, girls are more likely to be noticed for appearance and behavior.

Girls learn to be courteous. They apologize more than boys do and internalize criticism to a greater degree. Ask a boy about his problems in math and he will blame it on the teacher or another external factor; ask a girl and she will tend to take the blame herself. Though girls as a group work harder than boys do, they have less self-confidence. Girls are less assertive and more willing to stay within the boundaries. As athletes this makes girls more coachable, but they have to learn to be aggressive—a trait that is not always appreciated by their male counterparts.

Something happens to girls as they grow up. At age seven about 60 percent of girls are playing an organized sport. At age 16 about 30 percent are playing; by the senior year in high school the rate is down to 17 percent. There are a number of things working against girls. Like their male counterparts, they must deal with elitism—that is, only the best players survive to play on varsity teams. Girls begin to see sports as a threat to social relationships. Though girls are less violent and overt than boys, they still have the means to hurt, sometimes bullying with words or subtle slights. While girls bond more easily than boys do, they are also more deeply disappointed when a teammate lets them down. While the boy is rewarded with status, in some homophobic environments, girls are labeled as lesbians. They become concerned if their appearance becomes manly. Through it all society holds them to a higher standard of behavior—proper feminine etiquette.

The arena's a tough place for women; it's hardly a level playing field. Some 95 percent of TV sports are directed to men. College women have about one-third the athletic opportunity and scholarships that men are offered and about one-quarter the operating and recruiting budgets. In high school and college, women get leftover facilities, less practice time, and odd schedules for game times. While colleges argue that men's basketball and football are their big money makers, the truth is that the vast majority of these programs operate at a deficit.

What's a girl to do?

Will Women Change Sports, or Will Sports Change Women?

In 1970 only one out of twenty-seven girls played a sport in high school. Today that number is one in three. Eighty percent of U.S. high schools now have a girls' basketball program. Eighty-seven percent of parents agree that sports are important for boys *and girls*.

While women athletes continue to be judged by harsher appearance standards, that appears to be changing. Although nonathletic men continue to prefer Pamela Anderson types, athletic males now prefer more athletic-looking females. And that's a good thing. Cultural standards for women are totally unrealistic. The average American woman is five feet, four inches, and 142 pounds, but the average Miss America is five feet, nine inches, and 110 pounds—and 15 percent below the recommended body weight. No wonder 80 percent of 10-year-old girls don't like their bodies. It's an impossible standard. And the easiest way for a woman to get on the cover of *Sports Illustrated* is to wear a swimsuit.

Steroid use will especially tempt women, as their impact on a woman's performance is considerably more significant than for men.

That's changing. Girls are finding terrific role models in Mia Hamm, Cheryl Swoopes, Lisa Leslie, and Venus and Serena Williams. There's even an "Olympic Barbie"—probably a mixed blessing.

As women share a larger piece of the sports pie, they find themselves confronted with many of the same issues that have confronted men—often in a more virulent form. As professional opportunities and competition for scholarships increase, the quest for excellence will intensify. The same traits that make a woman a good athlete—drive, determination, and perfectionism—can lead to injury, eating disorders, and overbearing coaches. Steroid use will especially tempt women, as their impact on a woman's performance is considerably more significant than for men.

Will women develop their own unique sports, or will they challenge in traditionally male domains? There are about one thousand girls in high school football across the country, and girls are also participating in boxing and wrestling, raising numerous issues and challenges. Expect this trend to continue.

How should women approach the challenge?

⭐ 40 EMBRACE CHANGE

Both the culture and the sports world are changing at warp speed. The increasing presence of women in sports will continue to amaze as opportunities expand. Get used to it. The only thing constant will be change. Enjoy the ride.

Act As If You Belong

I came on active duty in the Army in 1974. In a class of 60 officers, there was one woman. I had never heard of such a thing, let alone actually seen a woman in uniform. The Army was in the process of phasing out the Women's Army Corps, which tended to segregate women in limited areas and career fields. Now there was one in our midst. It was mind-blowing.

I got over it.

The officer in question acted as if she belonged, and after a while she became one of us. I have seen this phenomenon many times since.

I've also seen what I call the double jeopardy phenomenon, a pecking order routine where women work in male-dominated areas. It goes like this: if a woman is good she gets double positives; if she's bad, she gets double negatives. It's not fair, but it's my observation. Women who are near the top of a male group are viewed as goddesses. They not only gain acceptance, they are revered. It's almost as if they can do no wrong. They tend to bond with the alpha males. If they have leadership qualities, they have a major influence over the group.

Are women gaining on men? By most objective measures, the answer is yes.

Unfortunately, the reverse is also true. Women near the bottom are stereotyped as sandbaggers, just taking advantage of the quota system. Whatever angst the men have is projected onto the weak sisters—even though there may be guys who are just as incompetent.

The middle ground is smaller for women—you're either one of the good ones or one of the bad ones. My advice in these situations—aim for the top. If you're looking for comfort near the bottom of the heap, you won't find any.

The military has opened a host of career opportunities to women, and we're not through yet. With each experience we keep finding that most of the problems we foresaw turned out to be bogeymen. The problems are almost always cultural. When the culture evolves, the problems are manageable.

Too often we fixate on the culture—namely, will the guys be able to handle it? I may be out of school here, but shouldn't the relevant question be, can the person do the job? If the answer is yes, then the culture must adapt to the situation. If that means ladies' rooms on submarines, so be it. The guys will just have to get used to it. Attitude adjustment is the military's strong suit; we can train to do about anything. And you can't tell me the United States of America can't afford ladies' rooms.

I've seen soldiers, men and women, dressing and undressing in the same tent. If they're busy enough and focused enough, it's not a problem. It's when they're bored that you start having problems. They start looking for things to fool around with. It's the leader's challenge to keep them busy on the mission.

The situation in the sports world is similar. I've seen women broadcasters trying to do their job in locker rooms full of naked baseball players. It's a little weird, but for the most part it seems to be working.

Do men have ego problems competing with women? Only when we lose. As long as we win it's not as big a problem.

Still, there is the male-domain thing. We like to think there are some things that only a man can do. When that's challenged, we feel bad. My answer to that is—so what? Go feel bad. If that makes you compete a little harder, that's fine. As long as you compete within the rules, load up.

I see this situation in youth wrestling. There are girls who routinely beat the boys. It's only devastating to the boys who've been brought up to think it's a disgrace to lose to a girl. The girls know when they go out there that the boys are going to load up on them. They accept it—it's part of the sport. Some folks worry about the body touching, but if you think about it, there's the same body touching with two boys, a state of affairs that would otherwise be socially unacceptable. It's all in how you look at it. Act like you belong—and come ready to rumble.

Understand as well that there are significant differences between the sexes. Men are generally taller and heavier; they have more upper-body strength and more lean muscle mass. We make good football players.

But the advantages are few. Men die on average seven years earlier and have a higher rate of suicide, heart attack, and stroke. Women are gifted with a better sensing ability, including better eyesight. They actually sweat more efficiently, are more flexible, and have greater ability to override pain. Men and women do about the same on stress tests.

Girls keep up with boys up to puberty, when the male hormones kick in. Girls mature sooner, with maximum growth at about age 12, a time when they can compete equally with boys, given the same training. The boys' hormones kick in around age 14, and they begin moving ahead in sports that favor size and strength. Most of our favorite sports reward those qualities.

Women have special maturation challenges. Ice skaters suffer when they develop hips and chests and lose some leaping ability; but women track and field stars peak relatively late, between ages 26 and 33. It's hard to say who the better athletes are in old age, because most of the men are dead. At least it seemed like we were ahead for a while.

Are women gaining on men? By most objective measures, the answer is yes. Just don't count the records of the former East Germans and Communist Chinese—believe me, those achievements are science, not sport. Minus steroid use, men will probably always have an edge in sports the culture fixates on. It's an interesting question, but it's not the most important one.

The more important issue is how we can encourage and sustain women's participation in sports and indeed harness the full range of women's contributions to society. We know that cultures that offer women freedom and opportunity outperform those that don't. Compare the United States, which has at least grappled with the tough gender issues, to any other country on Earth. Despite our imperfections, we are outperforming the rest of the world. Look at the cultures that stifle women and see how they're doing. They're not. And they won't be as successful until they stop limiting women and undergo a major, painful attitude adjustment.

Look at how U.S. women's teams have performed. Take soccer, a sport that evokes only moderate fan interest in the United States but that drives the rest of the world crazy with excitement. How is it our women have dominated the sport? The answer, very simply, is that they've finally been given the opportunity. That's not the case around the world. Given opportunity, our women have shown what they can do.

So act like you belong. Because you do.

TRAIN TOUGH CHALLENGE

- Continue to work to overcome the cultural challenges that face women in sports.

- Find a role model who fits your body type and plays your sport. Strive to be your best, but accept yourself too.

- U.S. women—continue to come through. The whole world's watching!

PART FIVE

ULTIMATE WEAPONS
MIND, BODY, AND SOUL

17

PLAN YOUR WORK; WORK YOUR PLAN

★

Set the example in physical fitness. It is a fact that physically fit people are mentally, physically, and emotionally stronger than people who are not. Physically fit people are better able to withstand stress in peace and war.
— ARMY FIELD MANUAL 22-100, *MILITARY LEADERSHIP*

For three years my son Jim wrestled at Park Hill High School in Kansas City, Missouri. In those three years I never saw a Park Hill wrestler lose a match because of conditioning. Without exception our kids were in better shape than our opponents. We won a lot of matches because we had more gas at the end.

This is you. This is where you need to be. You need to be the most supremely conditioned athlete on the face of the Earth. When the other guys are tuckered out, you'll still be going strong.

To get there you're going to have to plan your work, and work your plan.

Typical Jock Mentality: Guess we won't have time to get to the gym today.

Train Tough Attitude: OK, let's knock out some push-ups and sit-ups.

Got a Dream? Then Have a Plan

You supply the dream. Major league baseball? Varsity? The club championship? Leading the league in hitting? Bench pressing 250 pounds? Beating big sister in tennis?

How much time do you have? Ten years? A year? A month?

What are your midrange goals? When will you achieve them?

When you've answered these questions, you have a plan. You started with a dream; you laid out your dream over time. Then you established the goals you must meet en route to your dream and gave yourself deadlines for meeting the goals.

Planning is one of the most prized skills in the hierarchy of human endeavor, and you just took a crash course in it. If you actually took a piece of paper and stubby-penciled a plan, you placed yourself in the top 1 percent of Americans. Nobody plans to fail, but just about everybody fails to plan. You will soon be spanking the booties of a lot of players who don't plan.

What are you willing to give up in order to find more time, Mr. Busyman?

There are four elements that constitute an athlete's plan: training, conditioning, diet, and rest. Pretty simple.

But the element of time complicates things a bit. We all have a limited amount of time.

Please don't tell me you're busy. Because if you do, I will tell you that you are either unorganized, or worse, unmotivated. Just thinking about "too busy" hacks me off. So now I'm hacked off. So now I'm going to ask you a question. What are you willing to give up in order to find more time, Mr. Busyman?

Here are a few suggestions: television, video games, cell phones.

When I'm on a roll I cut way back on my TV time. I'll watch the ninth inning, the fourth quarter, and maybe the final holes of a golf tournament. Who needs all the rest? I never, ever play video games. I kept them out of the house for years, but now the kids are hooked. Not a problem for me, because 20 years ago I could see how they'd be a problem if I got involved. I'm not going to waste competitive juice killing Electronman. Don't need a cell phone. Don't want a cell phone. Like I really need a phone to tell my wife I'm turning into the driveway. I'm harder to get a hold of than Saddam Hussein. If I want ya, I'll call ya. Being inaccessible saves me a lot of time. Plus, my wife never knows when I'm turning into the driveway.

I hope this little rant has caused you to find a few things that habitually waste your time. I hope you can also see where your new found time can be applied to your plan to win.

So let's get back to the four basic elements of an athlete's training plan: training, conditioning, diet, and rest.

We'll take them one at a time.

Training

The single most important thing you can do is to play your sport. If you take nothing else from this chapter, play your sport. Play it as often as you can, against the best competition you can. Play with the big kids. Be a gym rat. Figure out how to stay on the floor. Run the gym. Become the leader. Get the playing time. Then find other gyms. Play over there too.

If you play your sport hard enough, you'll be in shape for it. You'll figure out what to eat for it, how much rest you should get for it. You learn a lot of things by playing your sport. Among the things you learn are the things you need to work on.

As long as we're talking about gyms, let's use basketball as an example. It's a great game.

Remember, in this chapter I'm primarily talking about your personal training plan.

Because I started going to basketball camp when I was six and attended every summer for 15 years, I consider myself a basketball player. In one form or another, I'm always playing basketball. Typically, I'm playing noontime ball in an Army gym. I never know who'll show up, but I know they'll be younger than I am. There's a prison on post, so we get a lot of guards on their off time. They usually arrive in a bad mood. In the summer we get the high school kids. Then there's the regular crowd, the guys who are in there day in and day out. The only way I can hang with these guys is to be on top of my game every day. I know I've got to get there early—and train.

> *Too many guys practice doing it incorrectly—and then it takes electroshock therapy to get them back on track.*

My training program has evolved over years of fine-tuning. It's designed to develop my skills in a finite amount of time using a finite amount of energy. If I train too long I won't have enough left for the competition.

The first thing I do is get there early. I want to be there before the other guys.

I stretch. I won't bore you with the details, other than to say that 80 percent of injuries are related to flexibility.

Then I dribble, an important skill for a point guard. I dribble around the gym a few times, being careful to keep my eyes focused on the various rims around the gym. I try to get the feel of bringing the ball down the floor like a ball handler.

Then I throw the ball against a concrete wall about 20 times with each hand. I find this loosens my shoulders—which have gotten a bit gimpy spiking volleyballs.

I start working on my inside game, shooting in close. I skip the head fakes—if you head fake in pickup games you just get hammered. The key is to get the ball up quickly, and that's what I work on.

Time for the free throw line. I've fine-tuned my free throw shooting, dissecting each element of the shot into its several hundred components. Each component has been practiced, become automatic, and been put back into the whole. I've got it down. The only thing I consciously think about now is cocking the wrist and getting a good ball rotation.

After I'm comfortable at the line, I practice midrange shooting. This also gives me time to rehearse my favorite moves, like the fallaway off a post-up. If guys have been stopping my standard moves, I invent something different and practice that for a while.

Whenever I'm a little winded I go back to the free-throw line.

Then it's straight-on 17-footers, followed by straight-on 20-footers. Along with free throws, I must be able to drill these shots. They're the shots we use to determine who plays when the gym gets crowded. We shoot free throws first and then move back from there. If you can't drill these shots, you don't play. That's why I practice them.

Finally, I bomb a few threes from a 45-degree angle before I look to join the other guys. I practice my side shots with the group, so they wind up rebounding for me. I'll get a good workout playing with these young stallions. So will they.

After the games, I'll find a corner of the gym for my push-ups and crunches. I'm always the first one there and the last one to leave—a lot of guys think I live at the gym.

Once a week I pay one of my kids to rebound for me so I can get my jump shot grooved.

I'm not going to the NBA, the CBA, or the WNBA. Guys who are need to be doing a lot more than I am. Kobe Bryant shoots 1,500 jump shots a day in the off-season. My goal is to effectively get it on with a random group of soldiers aged 18 to 48.

Whatever your goal is, you need to play your sport and have a plan. Make sure you're focusing your training plan on what's really impor-

41 SUPERCONDITION

Almost all world-class athletic achievement comes as a result of superconditioning. You can cover a lot of shortcomings with conditioning. Tailor your conditioning program to the sport you play, and learn the correct techniques for what you're doing. Commit to being in superior shape to your competition. It'll pay off when they quit and you're still pushing.

tant. Some 70 percent of all golf shots take place within 40 yards of the hole, yet most golfers spend 90 percent of their practice time with the driver, fairway woods, and long irons. It's easy to miss the point.

List the critical skills for your sport. Focus your plan on these skills, and be sure that what you're practicing is fundamentally sound. Too many guys practice doing it incorrectly—and then it takes electroshock therapy to get them back on track. Learn the fundamentals. Then head for the gym, the course, or whatever—and get to work.

Conditioning

You want to be in the best possible condition for your sport, and you want to tailor your conditioning program to your sport.

I absolutely believe in the benefits of superconditioning. That means finding ways to train harder and smarter than your competitors do. Almost all world-class athletic achievement comes as a result of superconditioning. Take former running back Walter Payton, for instance. Payton was one of the five greatest running backs of all time, though he played for the often-mediocre Chicago Bears. What made Walter Payton unique was the ferocity of his off-season conditioning program. He was always the most supremely conditioned athlete in the NFL, and it paid off in rushing production and injury-free seasons. The secret to Walter Payton's success was conditioning.

With any conditioning program, it's important to establish a base and keep yourself in the band of excellence.

You can cover a lot of shortcomings with conditioning. My sons placed third and fourth in the Kansas state wrestling program in their first year. Not only were they well coached, but they were supremely conditioned. They did push-ups, sit-ups, and wind sprints when they got up in the morning and more of the same when they got home from school. Then they went to practice. They may not have been the most experienced wrestlers in the state, but they were the best conditioned.

A word of caution here: while conditioning is important to athletic success, you want to be realistic about your body type and gear your efforts to what is achievable for you. There are football linemen body types and jockey body types, and it's a bit much to take one and try and mold him into the other. Women especially can get hung up on a quest for perfection, a situation that can lead to compulsive exercise and eating disorders.

But don't sell yourself short. For many years I was convinced that I was too small to make it in major league baseball. Then I had a very pleasant conversation with a big leaguer while he dressed for a game. I realized our bodies were almost identical. His name was Ozzie Smith, and he was one of the greatest shortstops to ever play the game. If you think you're "too this" or "too that," look around at successful athletes and you'll invariably find players with your body type who are doing the incredible. You can too.

Tailor your conditioning program to the sports you play. Invariably, this will include a mix of strength, flexibility, and endurance training. It may also include speed and agility training.

Athletes in all sports have recognized the benefits of weight training, whether accomplished with the Nautilus system, Universal weight lifting equipment, or free weights. I've used all three, and they can all be effective, but all rely on effective technique. Learn the correct technique first. The best way to do this is to hook up with a competent trainer. There are also a number of helpful books out there, complete with diagrams. Believe me, life is too short to do strength training without the right program and the proper technique. It's a lot of work either way; you might as well get something out of it. Here are some basics:

Warm up and stretch first. Get to at least a light sweat.
Work the large muscles first.
Lift and return weight slowly. Try for two seconds to lift and
    four seconds to return.
Inhale when bringing weight toward your body; exhale when
    moving weight away.

It's important to build up to peak performance, the time in your workout when you are in the flow and working to muscle failure, using your heavier weights. This is where you're making money. Let her rip. Then reduce the weight as you "work back down." Some trainers recommend you time your workouts and keep to a schedule to keep things moving. Most trainers agree that the optimal time of day for strength training is the first thing in the morning—but don't let the time of day keep you from a program.

Muscles need time to recover from training, usually 48 hours. Every other day is about right. During the off-season you might want to work out every day, doing upper body one day and lower body the next.

Keep push-ups and sit-ups in your repertoire, you can always do them when you can't get to your equipment or the gym. Learn the various types of push-ups and crunches—it's amazing what you can accomplish with no equipment at all.

Along with strength training, you need an aerobic workout and for most of us that means running. You run to build endurance, stamina, and wind. Running raises metabolism and burns off fat. Get a good pair of shoes, stretch, find a soft surface to run on if you need to lessen the effects of impact, and hit the road.

If you're looking for maximum effect in a shorter amount of time, consider wind sprints. Not only do you get the aerobic effects of running, but you lengthen your stride and increase foot speed. Try sprinting 100 yards at 75 percent speed and jogging the return distance at a slow pace. Start with 6 repetitions and add a rep for successive workouts up to 12.

With any conditioning program, it's important to establish a base and keep yourself in the band of excellence. Even when you're in a down period—and all of us have them—don't let yourself go to the point where you're essentially starting over. You lose 80 percent of conditioning after four weeks of inactivity. It will take a month of busting your butt to get it back.

Sprinkle variety into everything you do. You'll get bored and burn out if you try and do the same thing in every workout. I have about

---

★ **42 STAY IN THE BAND OF EXCELLENCE**

With any conditioning program, it's important to establish a base and keep yourself in the band of excellence. Even when you're in a down period—and all of us have them—don't let yourself get to the point where you have to start over. Find the time to do what needs to be done. Use simple exercises, like push-ups and sit-ups, to keep you grounded.

---

a dozen different anaerobic and aerobic workouts, and I'm always looking for more. When it snows I cross-country ski; when the lake freezes over I'm out there skating. I find new exercises by experimenting and also by watching what the other guys are doing. You can find a dozen or more workout books in your public library. It wouldn't hurt to subscribe to a fitness magazine either—just something to tweak your interest each month and give you a motivational boost and some fresh ideas. You want a dynamic program—always expanding, stimulating, and efficient.

Diet

Common sense. Common sense. Common sense. These are Bender's three rules of diet.

There are a million diet plans out there, and most of them are worth considering. But some of them don't pass the commonsense test. If it sounds funny to you, it probably is.

Stick to basics. Three meals a day. A good breakfast along with a multivitamin. A sampling of the basic food groups. Reasonable portions. Obviously you adjust if you need to gain or lose weight. Otherwise you can go with what you learned in eighth-grade health class.

Establish good eating habits. Habits are the key. Keep the good ones; destroy the bad ones. Eat slowly. Chew your food. Wipe your mouth. Help with the dishes.

Avoid junk food. If you're addicted it will take three days of going cold turkey to clean up. You'll have the craving all three days, but afterward, you'll be fine—and you'll have destroyed a bad habit.

> *Half of establishing a healthy diet is getting rid of bad habits; the other half is establishing good ones.*

As mentioned earlier, alcohol adds calories, slows metabolism, and will make you hungry—along with lowering your resolve. Drink in moderation or not at all.

Be especially careful about what you eat on game day. You want an empty stomach while you play; you want to be hungry. The lion only hunts when it's hungry, and you'll play better if you don't have to carry a full stomach. Try to eat four hours before game time, and eat things you know you digest easily. Forget the pregame steak; that's the last thing you need to be carrying. Think chicken or pasta in a light sauce.

Half of establishing a healthy diet is getting rid of bad habits; the other half is establishing good ones. One of the easiest habits to adopt is to increase your daily water intake. Your body needs plenty of water to transport nutrients and carbohydrates, as well as to help your kidneys clear the blood of waste products and toxins. When your water intake is low, you feel sluggish, as your body struggles to process energy in a polluted environment.

Drink a lot of water, and drink it often—10 eight-ounce glasses a day is about right. You'll find you look and feel better. Water keeps your eyes clear and your skin and hair healthy looking. Drinking water can also help control appetite. Drink a glass before a meal and another as you eat. Many times we feel we're hungry when we're

---

43 KICK BAD HABITS; REPLACE WITH GOOD

Half of establishing a healthy diet is getting rid of bad habits; the other half is establishing good ones. Apply common sense, along with the basics of what you recall from eighth-grade health class. Drink more water; get more rest. Out with the bad habits, in with the good.

actually thirsty. Don't wait until you feel thirsty to drink. Thirst indicates that dehydration is already taking place. Dehydration affects the brain, causing headaches and negatively affecting mood. So drink up!

Rest

About 20 years ago the Army realized we had a problem. Our leaders were wearing themselves out. Guys would go out on a 72-hour field exercise and stay awake the entire time. It was considered the manly thing to do. By the end of the third day they were walking into trees and making stupid decisions. Then they "crashed" and were essentially worthless for 24 hours while they caught up on their Zs. That's a heckuva way to run a war. All the bad guys had to do was attack on the fourth day.

After several studies and the expenditure of your tax dollars, we confirmed that if we didn't sleep, we got tired. We decided we needed a sleep plan. So now, while some leaders are directing the battle, the other leaders are resting. Sure, we can peak when we have to, but if we stick with the plan, we won't collapse just as we're putting a stranglehold on the bad guys.

You need a sleep plan too. Studies show that just a half-hour less than optimal sleep makes for a bad day. Check out how little brother plays the day after he has a sleepover at his friend's house. You know it—he's toast.

The older you get, the more you appreciate sleep. Unfortunately, the younger you are, the more sleep you need. Everybody's different, and you have to find out what *you* really need. Start with eight hours and figure from there.

If you're a traveling athlete, you also need to know the effects of catnaps. Some players benefit greatly from the ability to snooze; for others it just upsets their nighttime sleep. Whatever your sleep profile, have a plan to get what you need. Recognize that you'll be keyed up the night before games as well as immediately after night games. Learn how to calm yourself down. Have a calming bedtime routine. Go to bed when you're tired—not after late-night TV. Cut off caffeine intake early in the day. And of course, get plenty of exercise.

Learn how to rest—during the day, during exercise, even during the game. Stay off your feet the day of the game. Take advantage of time-outs to completely relax. Lie down between contests. Change socks and jocks. Completely chill. Give your body a chance to rejuvenate . . . so it will be there for you when it's time to attack.

TRAIN TOUGH CHALLENGE

- Stop wasting time. Have a plan.

- Play your sport. Play with the big kids.

- Get in the best possible physical shape for your sport.

- Understand what you eat and why. Drink plenty of water. Show up hungry.

- Plan your rest. Have a sleep plan. Allow your body to rejuvenate.

18

THE HYPER STATE

★

The voice of battle hurtled in the air,
Horses did neigh, and dying men did groan,
And ghosts did shriek and squeal about the streets.
— WILLIAM SHAKESPEARE, FROM *JULIUS CAESAR*

Do you ever feel angry?

Do you sometimes feel like you've been cheated, that the guy across town has it better, that his girlfriend is cuter, that his car and clothes are nicer than yours?

Do you have a temper? Does your dad have a temper? Your mom?

Do you watch the World Wrestling Federation or World Championship Wrestling and say, "Gee, I wish I could do that"?

Do you find it upsetting when kick-off and punt-return artists run sideways instead of full steam ahead? Or when a receiver drops a pass because he might be hearing footsteps?

Are there guys in the big leagues, NFL, or NBA that you just can't stand?

Do you hate stupid psychological questions? Am I striking a chord here?

If the answer to any of these questions is "Yes," you're definitely a candidate for the hyper state.

Of course, you might not want to go to the hyper state, even if you qualify. The hyper state is not without its dangers. It can be hazardous to other people's health. It's not nice. It's not polite. And it can backfire. Handling explosives is not for everybody. You might be better off in counseling.

On the other hand, the hyper state can be *cathartic*, our vocabulary word for this chapter. That means it can be a cleansing experience, a healthy way to burn off rage in a society that otherwise discourages repeated acts of mayhem and carnage.

Typical Jock: These guys are going to be tough.
Train Tough Attitude: These guys are going to be toast.

Hyper State University

I thought I was attending Wheaton College, a small liberal arts college outside Chicago. In reality, I had enrolled at Hyper State University. The dean of admissions at Hyper State was a kid named Al Davis, not to be confused with the Al Davis of Oakland Raiders fame—although the two are a lot alike. Al grew up in the rough-and-tumble world of Philadelphia, where he lettered in football, basketball, and baseball. A handsome Italian, Al had a compact body made of steel—he was a little guy you knew not to mess with. Al was wound tight, a ticking time bomb, always set to go off. Picture Al Pacino screaming "Attica!"in *Dog Day Afternoon*—that was Al.

He was a year ahead of me in college, and it was obvious from the start that Al was going to be the leader and I was going to be taking notes. I thought I was a pretty competitive guy, but that was only because I hadn't met Al. Despite the fact that I was a couple of inches taller, I soon was calling him by his favorite moniker: "Big Al."

Big Al was a gamesman extraordinaire. He could beat you 11 ways to Sunday. Al grew up playing all the games in Philly—which he would teach me so he could enjoy beating me at each of them.

Our favorite was floor hockey. We played with plastic equipment on the attic floor in a mansion where Al "worked." Whenever the missus was away, the attic became the Philadelphia Spectrum where we went at it tooth and nail. One guy fired the puck while the other guy played goalie, complete with ski goggles, baseball mitt, and protective cup. I had played some hockey with my dad on the frozen lakes of Ohio, so I was familiar with a hockey stick and could hold my own—even with Big Al.

This was a big deal. Before each game Al would sing both the U.S. and Canadian national anthems. He kept up a running commentary on every play, complete with mammoth postscore celebrations. By the end of a series we were both ringing wet, thoroughly drenched from the orgy of competition. I was often ahead, but I don't remember ever winning a championship series. Like the Incredible Hulk, Al had the ability to shift into another gear at crunch time, to attain a state of overwhelming frenzy.

> *Al had the ability to shift into another gear at crunch time, to attain a state of overwhelming frenzy.*

This hyper state seemed an extension of Al's personality. It melded enthusiasm and confidence with an insatiable drive to win. At the time, Muhammad Ali, Julius Erving, and Pete Rose exhibited similar abilities in the professional ranks. But it was one thing to watch it on TV and quite another to take it on in somebody's attic.

I didn't know exactly what it was or what caused it, but I knew one thing—when I grew up, I wanted to be just like Al.

My Hyper State Diploma

Most athletes have something that distinguishes them from other similar athletes—something they just have and don't know why. It might be jumping ability, a great arm, the ability to take pain, foot speed, strength, quickness, toughness, determination, reactions, eyesight, hands—any number of gifts, great or small. Sometimes that gift is bigger than you think. Sometimes it can be parlayed into something even bigger.

About the time I turned 30, I was assigned to Fort Benjamin Harrison, Indiana. Fort Harrison was a beehive of sports activities at the time, and because my instructor duties were fairly light, I was involved in all of them.

For the first time in my life, I got into competitive running. As a serious baseball player, track and field had never been an option. But at Harrison, I found time to do it all. I competed in everything from 100 meters to half-marathons. I tried the 400, the 800, the mile, the two mile, and 5- and 10-Ks.

I wasn't about to be invited to the Olympic trials, but I did find that I had a special gift—the ability to perform down the stretch of a race. For some unknown reason, if I could feel another runner as we approached the finish, I could find another gear and blow by him. It didn't matter how tired I was or how much pain was present. It was an animal thing. If I could smell someone in the last 100 meters, they were toast. My mind would go blank, pain and discomfort would shut off, and I would feel myself propelled forward—almost as if I was being sucked to the finish line by a giant vacuum. If you've ever been on a horse that bolts for the barn, that was me. It was very much like a dream, where the only fear was that my legs would continue accelerating to the point where they would melt or come off. It was my first experience in the hyper state, and it was terrifying. This wasn't about being in the zone. This was about being in a whole new universe.

When we played West Point, it was a war.

It got worse. It started spreading to other sports. Remember, I'm at Fort Harrison where sports were king. And now I'm playing volleyball. Volleyball was a sport that I picked up in college gym class, played a lot in California, and eventually played with the Germans and Dutch over in Europe. In many ways it was the perfect sport for me. I love reaction games that test hand-eye coordination and timing and have lots of jumping around. If you asked me what my favorite sport is, I'd probably say volleyball.

But it wasn't until Fort Harrison that I really got focused. Someone pointed out that I was jumping off one foot for spikes, a typical problem for guys that play a lot of basketball. No wonder I wasn't getting any power on my hits. Once I made that little correction, I was a whole new volleyball player. I started using visualization to get ready for each game. My focus times were awesome.

We played all over town and then traveled to an end-of-season tournament against Army teams from across the nation. I was jacked up. The same thing that happened at the end of a race was starting to happen in volleyball. I simply lost all fear—and all restraint. I was taking guys on at the net with a vengeance. If they wanted to get it on, it was fine with me. I was looking them in the eye, daring them to come on. My spikes were vicious, and I could cut my hits different ways to keep the blockers off balance. And then, when they least expected it, the dink. I was on fire.

Our team broke down door after door until we found ourselves in a new dimension.

Oddly, it was a facial that finally demonstrated just how far into the hyper zone I had journeyed. We were playing West Point, a team I naturally disliked. They not only had better financial backing then any of the other teams, they had an attitude to go with it. When we played West Point, it was a war.

Midway through the final game, one of their monsters spiked a ball down the net. I was in the front row, in a dig position. I never saw the ball. It struck me full in the face and caromed high over the net, still in play. It was all so fast, no one knew what happened. People in the stands told me later that they assumed the ball hit my shoulder, because no one could survive a blow like that to the face. I never flinched. Involuntary tears stung my eyes, and my face turned what I'm sure was a deep crimson, but I never missed a beat. I took the shot of my life as though it were a walk in the park. Rod Serling, of *Twilight Zone* fame, whispered in my ear. I was out there somewhere in the "outer limits." And frighteningly, it was beginning to feel a lot like home.

But it wasn't until softball season that I got my hyper state diploma, with "Big Al" on hand for the occasion. He was visiting from Chicago where he was a successful high school coach, a profession he would soon practice in the college ranks.

The Harrison softball team was a motley crew—mostly enlisted soldiers, with a couple marine recruiters thrown in to complete the madness. We played weekend tournaments with some success getting ready for an Army tournament at Fort Eustis, Virginia.

The week before we were leaving for Virginia, we played a local tournament in Indianapolis. We lost to a group of pretty boys early on and spent most of the weekend trying to battle our way out of the losers' bracket. It wasn't until Sunday afternoon that we realized that we'd be facing the same group of pretty boys that beat us the first time around. We'd have to beat them twice to win the championship.

For some reason, I didn't like those guys. I never saw a group of guys so in love with themselves. Their whole manner pretty much said what they thought: "We're better than you, and you should be honored to be on the same field with us." They spent most of the afternoon sunning themselves, watching us slave out of the losers' bracket. By the time we met them for the championship, we'd already played five Sunday games to their one. We had every reason to bow to their apparent superiority and just phone it in. But something told me that if we could get these guys dirty, we could beat them.

I got fired up. It started innocently enough, just by taking an extra base and sliding hard. But then I started agitating, stirring up my teammates, projecting energy I wasn't supposed to have that late in the day. Maybe it was the heat, but things started talking to me, telling me to lead my team out of the wilderness. I wanted to win this war in a fight to the finish, and only one way made sense—attack, attack, attack.

We took game one in a come-from-behind victory.

By nightfall things were getting ugly, both teams jawing back and forth. But now we had them dirty, right where they didn't want to be. There was no way these guys were going to hang with the group of ghetto graduates, gunslingers, and country boys we had assembled. Their "above the fray" attitude was in ashes. Meanwhile, our whole team was playing out of the hyper zone—and we weren't coming back without the win.

At one point I must have miscued a ball at third. Man, did the pretty boys dog me out. But I was way too involved to be distracted. Their power hitter tried to knock me into left field on the next pitch, but I robbed him and doubled off the runner at first. It was that way all night—two teams going at it like dogs fighting over a bone. Our team broke down door after door until we found ourselves in a new dimension. It was a fight to the finish, and when the finish came, we were there and they weren't.

Afterward, Big Al and I beat a hasty retreat. I felt as if I had just been through a battle. It was only then that the depth of the carnage began to sink in. It shook me up and—frankly—scared the heck out of me. But I felt a lot better when Al told me such feelings were quite normal—in a bona fide graduate of Hyper State.

Above the Zone

We hear a lot about being "in the zone," that place where everything clicks, where we find a place of focus and quiet concentration. But is there a place that's *above* the zone? A place that lifts performance to an even higher plane?

I maintain that there is—because I've been there. It's travel to a new dimension, to a place that will change your life forever. It's always a wild ride.

The biochemical transition alone is enough to produce time warp: blood pressure rises, deep breathing saturates the blood with oxygen, and the heart shifts into overdrive—priming muscles that will be called upon to do the impossible. The adrenal gland kicks in. The brain's synapses fire more quickly; there is a sense of creative exhilaration—that somehow we will find a way.

It's the final gear in our human gearbox, and it takes a bit of jiggling the clutch to get us there. Blind rage always works for me, with a bit of vengeance thrown in for good measure. I get angry. These aren't normally your most saintly qualities, but remember, we're talking about a contest here, not an interpersonal relationship. Still, this kind of thinking is not for everyone.

And not everyone will be comfortable there.

Can one be too keyed up . . . or peak too soon? Of course.

Couldn't drugs take one to the hyper state? Yes, but that would be cheating.

Many athletes perform better in a quiet normalcy, and most sports situations call for just that. But others of us, in the right situation, take that walk on the wild side, where total abandon rules.

The Hyper Home Workout

Have you ever been at a roller rink when the music heats up and the skaters keep accelerating until they're out of control? Or you're cruising the highway to your favorite tune before realizing you're going 105 mph?

Music is a great way to set a mood, and therefore an easy route to the hyper zone. Try this.

Set up a private area complete with your favorite workout toys: dumbbells, barbells, whatever. Find your most raucous CD, put it in your music machine, and crank up the volume. Now get to work.

The hyper home workout will take you to a place you've never been before—the hyper zone. You can be totally off the wall in the hyper zone. Stay hyped between sets; this is the time to work on your most radical dance moves. It should be easy to exceed your normal workout reps by 20 percent. Push yourself to the limit—it's time to break through to the other side. Imagine what it will be like when you hit the floor at your next game—or at the next party. You'll be on fire!

Plus, your hyper home workout will give you some idea of what it's like to perform in the hyper zone—and what it takes to get there.

The Hyperization of Bob

My son Bob marches to the beat of a different drummer. In fact, he doesn't march at all, he kind of shuffles. Bob's not into traditional sports, probably as a result of yours truly, the Great Santini, crowding his space. Bob's into skateboarding and snowboarding—and that's fine. He was also a darned good wrestler.

Bob finished third in Kansas Kids' Wrestling his first year in the sport at age seven. What he did that year was incredible.

Unfortunately for Bob, we spent the next four years in Europe where we were unable to find a kids' wrestling program. When we

44 HYPE OUT

Use the hyper home workout to give you an idea of what it's like to perform in the hyper zone. Set up a private area with your favorite workout toys: dumbells, barbells, whatever. Find your most raucous CD, and crank up the volume. Now get to work. Exceed your normal workout by 20 percent.

returned to the States, Bob took up the sport again, but of course he had slipped far behind his peers. We expected that, but getting repeatedly thumped in the sport of wrestling is never fun.

Kids' wrestling is a huge investment of time and energy for parents, coaches, and kids. Tournaments take place on Saturdays and are scattered far and wide across the state. Weigh-ins start at 6:00 A.M., and meets often last all day and into the night. It's no place for half-hearted commitment.

At one point, that's all Bob seemed to be giving. He'd been pinned by a kid I thought he could hold his own against, putting in a lackluster performance. The kid was the only wrestler in Bob's weight class that day, so we faced the unpleasant prospect of waiting around four hours so he could wrestle the kid again. I was darned if he was going to wrestle the kid the same way a second time.

At the time I was reading Pat Riley's *The Warrior Within*, so there was no shortage of motivational material available. I kept feeding Bob the highlights throughout the afternoon, psyching him up for a dog-fight. At that point I just wanted to see some dog.

Bob didn't disappoint. He attacked that kid in ways that surprised even himself. Savagery will take you only so far in wrestling; at some point finesse and technique begin to rule the day. But Bob broke down the door to a new dimension that afternoon. He was back.

I witnessed two different wrestlers that day; the first was a see-what's-gonna-happen novice, and the second was a wild dog fighting for a bone. That dog became Bob's best friend, and from then on he brought him hungry to every meet.

45 GET HYPED

Agitate. Project energy. Go over the top, above the zone, and into the hyper state. Attack. Attack. Attack!

Over the Top

"Over the top" has become a cute way of describing the antics of many pop music groups on the scene today. That's not what it used to mean. "Over the top" referred to the act of a soldier in World War I departing the relative security of a trench to cross no-man's-land and attack the enemy. It was a lethal endeavor. Most of those guys never came back, and those who did were seldom the same. The act itself was one of supreme courage, usually involving an officer or sergeant leading the way. There are those who said it was a stupid way to fight, that the sacrifice was too great for the ground gained. But at the time, it was the way men fought.

Going over the top, above the zone, and into the hyper state will not be for everyone. It is not without risk. But as long as men fight to win, they will journey into the hyper state.

Get up out of that trench. Follow the sergeant into no-man's-land. Be thankful there aren't any machine guns on a football field. Attack!

TRAIN TOUGH CHALLENGE

- Look for situations where the hyper state might boost your performance.

- Practice with the hyper home workout.

- Perform with abandon. Let out the dog!

19

NEVER, EVER GIVE UP

★

"They've got us surrounded again, the poor bastards."
—GENERAL CREIGHTON ABRAMS, AT THE BATTLE OF THE BULGE

Winston Churchill, Great Britain's prime minister during World War II, was the stuff of legend—and most of the legends are true. But, as it turns out, one of my favorite Churchill stories is actually a bit of an embellishment.

At the end of his career, Churchill revealed that, "it was my ambition all my life to be master of the spoken word." And master he was, perhaps the greatest orator in history.

So it was with great anticipation that an assembled audience waited for the prime minister's speech. The date was October 29, 1941—deep in the dark days of World War II. The site was Harrow School, which Churchill had attended as a boy.

After a lengthy introduction, Churchill stepped to the lectern and spoke but four words: "Never, ever, give up," he said, and sat back down.

A surprised headmaster asked Mr. Churchill if he perhaps had something to add.

"Never give in," he said, "never, never, never, never." And he returned to his seat.

That's the legend, and were that all Churchill said that day, it would have summed up his life philosophy. Churchill was a bulldog. He looked like a bulldog, and he had the same basic attitude. Once he got his teeth into something, he never let go.

This was a man who rose to lead England after taking the blame for one of his country's biggest blunders—the Gallipoli landings in World War I. "Success," Churchill believed, "is the ability to go from one failure to another with no loss of enthusiasm."

The fact is, Churchill had much more to say that day.

"Never yield to force," he advised. "Never yield to the apparently overwhelming might of the enemy."

Good Question: Why a military perspective on sports?

Train Tough Attitude: It's an attitude, Baby, a way to get things done.

A Military Mind

Why do I advocate a military mentality on the sports field? Because it takes advantage of a deeper drive, that's why. Sometimes as athletes we start to think we're the center of the universe. And we're not. Not even close. We need to get some perspective. We need to recognize a higher power and a higher calling. We need to hear the voices of the leaders who took on the impossible so we could be free.

Let's stick with the Winston Churchill example, and you'll see what I mean.

When I want the real thing, I always go back to Winnie.

Let's go back to the early days of World War II.

Germany had fallen into the evil clutches of the charismatic Adolf Hitler and his Nazi henchmen. Spewing his unique brand of racism, Hitler was hell-bent on extending Nazi power in western Europe and the world. He had rebuilt the German military and begun his strategy of conquest. The countries fell like dominoes: Austria, Czechoslovakia, Poland, Denmark, Norway, Holland, Belgium.

The Germans rolled over western Europe with a new military strategy called "blitzkrieg," or lightning warfare. They used close air support and mobile tank warfare to fight their way around the French Maginot Line. The French were routed in six weeks. Their fleet was captured; they didn't even fight for Paris. We still use the term *blitz* in football when the linebackers rush the quarterback. But the real blitz was even scarier.

Miraculously, the British Expeditionary Force escaped France and ferried across the English Channel to England in small boats. "We must be careful not to assign to this deliverance the attributes of victory," Churchill warned. "Wars are not won by evacuations."

Britain stood alone. The United States had not yet entered the war. They prepared for a German invasion that would surely come. German warplanes began dropping bombs indiscriminately on British cities, killing and maiming civilians and reducing a historic past to rubble.

But Churchill made it clear that the British would fight a far more tenacious battle than the French had. "We have not journeyed across the centuries, across the oceans, across the prairies, because we are made of sugar candy," he said.

These are the words he gave to the British people as they faced the darkening storm:

> The whole fury and might of the enemy must very soon be turned on us. Hitler knows that he will have to break us in this Island or lose the war. If we can stand up to him, all Europe may be free and the life of the world may move forward into broad, sunlit uplands. But if we fail, then the whole world, including the United States, including all that we have known and cared for, will sink into the abyss of a new Dark Age made more sinister, and perhaps more protracted, by perverted science. Let us therefore brace ourselves to our duties, and so bear ourselves that, if the British Empire and its Commonwealth last for a thousand years, men will still say, "This was their finest hour."

Have you ever performed for your team or school knowing it could be your finest hour? I hope that someday you'll have that chance. Can you imagine what it's like to play with that kind of attitude? To con-

46 AIM FOR YOUR FINEST HOUR

Can you imagine what it's like to play with a finest-hour attitude? To convey the attitude that you'll never quit and never give in? Imagine what kind of message that sends to the other team? It's almost crazy. It's the attitude that gets you back up when you've been knocked down, that keeps you on the field when the others are showing those subtle signs of quitting. It's being tough-minded and believing you can overcome any obstacle.

vey the attitude that you'll never quit and never give in? Imagine what kind of message that sends to the other team? It's almost crazy. It's the attitude that gets you back up when you've been knocked down, that keeps you on the field when the others are showing those subtle signs of quitting. It's being tough-minded and believing you can overcome any obstacle.

Winston Churchill wasn't a god, but he thought like one. He was just as human as you or I. At the time of World War II he was thought to be past his prime, a roly-poly chap who walked with a cane and sported a bow tie. He was photographed in a series of rather ridiculous hats.

But he had a great puss.

And he wasn't afraid to get out among the people who were making the real sacrifices. He had the look. His presence inspired confidence. His famed "V for Victory" hand sign gave hope to millions.

And Churchill had a vision. Read his words and see if you get the idea:

We have but one aim and irrevocable purpose. We are resolved to destroy Hitler and every vestige of the Nazi regime. From this nothing will turn us—nothing. We will never parley. We will never negotiate with Hitler or any of his gang. We shall fight him by land. We shall fight him by sea. We shall fight him in the air, until with God's help we have rid the earth of his shadow and liberated its people from his yoke.

"That was worth 1,000 guns, and the speeches of 1,000 years," wrote one Brit after listening to Churchill. Sixty years later, his words still send a chill down my spine and make my hair stand on end. I carry his words with me on three-by-five-inch cards.

Knute Rockne, Vince Lombardi, Bill Parcells, Lou Holtz, Pat Riley—I've got them all down on three-by-five-inch cards. But when I want the real thing, I always go back to Winnie.

What Churchill Said About Slumps

When I was 13, Mickey Mantle reached down into his travel bag and pulled out a roughed-up baseball. "To the Bender Boys—Best wishes on my 469th H.R." he wrote on it. It was August 1965, and Mickey was on a crusade to reach 500 career home runs. He would finish with 536—along with another 18 homers in World Series competition.

It was a career that almost never happened—because in 1951 Mickey Mantle almost quit. His rookie season with the Yankees had gone poorly. Vaunted as "the next Joe DiMaggio," expectations were high, and Mantle failed to live up to them. He struck out, misplayed balls in the outfield, and found himself mired in a slump. The New York press and fans were tough on him, as were his teammates. Casey Stengel, the legendary Yankees manager, sent him to the Kansas City Blues, at the time the Yankees' Triple-A farm club.

The slump continued. Feeling lonesome and feeling the pressure, Mickey lost his desire to play in the big leagues. His bat lost its pop. Once known for his towering drives, he now looked more like a "banjo hitter," hitting weak ground balls and pop-ups.

The slump bottomed out with a soul-staggering 0–21 stretch. Mickey called his dad from Kansas City and told him, "I just can't

---

47 RETURN TO SIMPLE ACTION

When things get tough, start doing the little things right. Focus on executing each fundamental with single-point attention. Let go of results. Do each step of the process to the very best of your ability—and stay positive.

play anymore." Mickey's dad was a coal miner from Commerce, Oklahoma. His dream was to see Mickey make it in the major leagues and escape the coal mines that would eventually curtail his own life. Mickey's dad made the five-hour drive to Kansas City.

Return to simple action.

That night the father-son team worked through the problem. By Mickey's account it was not a fun process. The turning point seemed to come when the senior Mantle offered: "You can always work in the mines with me." Mickey's choices were pretty simple: make it as a ballplayer, or head home with Dad—where his prospects were limited.

Something clicked.

The next night Mantle and the Blues played in my hometown of Toledo, Ohio, against the Mud Hens. It was before my time, but my dad was on hand to see the slumping phenom. "A pimply faced kid," was how my dad always described his first look at the kid from Commerce.

We'd be seeing a lot more of that kid.

That night Mickey broke out of his slump. He hit a triple and a double and drove two home-run balls over the light towers at Swain Field. In his final at-bat, the third baseman was playing back, probably in fear for his life, and Mickey bunted—to hit for the cycle.

Over the next 40 games Mantle went on a tear: 11 home runs, 50 RBI, batting for a .361 average.

By August he was back with the Yankees.

The father-son Mantle team probably knew of Winston Churchill only as a great wartime leader, but they acted in perfect sync with one of Churchill's great admonitions.

"In critical and baffling situations," he said, "it is always best to return to first principle and simple action."

First principle for the Mantles was crystal clear—escape the mines. Parlay Mickey's physical gifts and make him a major league baseball player. Their father-son relationship was based on doing the hard work required to make that dream a reality. For a time, mired in the depth of a slump, Mickey lost that vision. But when he returned to first principle, he returned with a vengeance.

Simple action is the other key to slump busting—with the emphasis on "simple."

What happens to a good hitter who stops hitting the ball? He's out of sync. He loses focus. Something gets him off track. It could be overconfidence, fatigue, the party life, the opposition exploiting a weakness—any number of things. The once-esteemed batting average goes down. Confidence suffers. The downward spiral begins, seemingly out of control.

Slumps are perpetuated when we start doing the little things wrong. Slumping hitters are almost always swinging at bad pitches. One of the disciplines that make a good hitter in the first place is pitch selection. But in his haste to make something happen, the hitter loses sight of this important fundamental. Now he's taking pitches down the middle and swinging at stuff that's eye-high. Panic sets in. The way out is lost. What to do?

> *Do each step of the process to the very best of your ability—and stay positive.*

Return to simple action. Start doing the little things right. Focus on executing each fundamental with single-point attention. Let go of results. Do each step of the process to the very best of your ability—and stay positive.

Get your act together in the on-deck circle.
Stride to the plate with confidence.
See the ball.
Pick a good pitch.
Grounded out? At least you hit it.
Line drive right at somebody? Hey, you hit it square.
Texas leaguer that fell for a hit? A hit's a hit.
First principle and simple action.

And it's the same whether you're struggling on the golf course, at the free throw line, or in the great game of life.

Mickey Mantle summed it up pretty well in the printed message on that 469th home-run ball he gave my brother and me: "Keep Swingin'."

There Are No Safe Battles

"Success cannot be guaranteed," Churchill was fond of saying. "There are no safe battles."

The generals who longed for a tidy battlefield were seldom successful. Every operation carried risk—to soldiers, to reputations, and to the ultimate success of the war. But the alternative was a slow, agonizing defeat. And successful leaders took calculated risks in pursuit of the ultimate goal—winning the war.

Military units are kind of like football teams—they take on the characteristics of their leaders. Nowhere was this more apparent than in the final months of World War II.

The Germans surprised us in their last massive offensive of the war—throwing everything they had at us in the Battle of the Bulge. The U.S. 101st Airborne clung tenaciously to a critical road juncture at Bastogne, deep in the Ardennes Forest of Belgium. The attacking Germans quickly surrounded the Americans and demanded their surrender.

General Anthony McAuliffe sent out a one-word response: "Nuts."

The Americans hung on.

General George Patton volunteered to swing his Third Army north to relieve his beleaguered comrades. When asked how long it would take to get there, Patton replied, "48 hours."

No one believed him.

---

48 EXPECT A FEW SMACKS IN THE EYE

"There are no safe battles," said Winston Churchill. Success depends on taking calculated risks in the face of adversity. You're going to get knocked down and smacked around. Expect it. Soldier through it, and counterattack. The reward for painful, relentless effort is victory.

But Patton already had a plan, and his forces were trained for lightning-quick operations.

They had also taken on the audacious personality of their leader. They burst through the German defenses to link with the 101st. The German party was over.

The reward for selfless, relentless effort was victory—and the difficult task of reshaping the world in concert with a belligerent Soviet Union.

Even in victory Churchill saw the difficulties ahead. On the day World War II ended, he said simply, "We may allow ourselves a brief period of rejoicing."

Today Winston Churchill's formal speeches are published in eight volumes—some 50,000 pages. They occupy more than two feet of shelf space. The man who saved England, and perhaps our democratic way of life, achieved his goal of mastering the spoken word. And you can't fully appreciate perseverance in the face of adversity until you know something of the life of Winston Churchill. And now you know.

Churchill never dunked a basketball or drove the ball out of the park, but he communicates to athletes the same way he communicated to his struggling countrymen.

"A young man cannot expect to get very far in life," he said, "without some good smacks in the eye."

TRAIN TOUGH CHALLENGE

- Go to the library. Look for a book called *Churchill: A Life* by Martin Gilbert. Read it if you want to, but at least look at the pictures. Check out Winston Churchill in action.

- When things are tough, return to your first principle.

- When the failures pile up, take action—simple action.

- Never give up. Never give in.

20

DEFEAT INTO VICTORY

★

Wars may be fought by weapons, but they are won by men. It is the spirit of the men who follow and the man who leads that gains victory.

—GENERAL GEORGE PATTON

Some things are under our control, while others are not under our control.

—EPICTETUS

To be an athlete is to be a philosopher. It comes with the territory. It's not the wins that turn us philosophic; it's those darned losses. Sooner or later they happen to every athlete, to every team. And they have to be dealt with; hence, philosophy.

Philosophy is the study of the principles and thought processes that govern a field of knowledge or an activity—such as the philosophy of sport. It's our philosophy that provides the system of morals, character, and behaviors that get us through the tough times of injury, embarrassment, and defeat—and that keeps us coming back with renewed energy.

Our personal philosophy helps us address the tough questions—such as, why sports? Why all the time and energy devoted to an artificial activity?

Each of us has to answer that question for ourselves.

For me, the answer has never been a completely rational one. I don't know what drives me. Ego? Testosterone? Upbringing? The warrior spirit?

I do know that sports provide a sense of finality not often found in life. Winning and losing is often undefined in the day-to-day. In sports, it's pretty obvious.

There's something engaging about all-out effort in pursuit of a goal. Something about using our bodies—not phone calls, E-mails, and briefings—to carry out the task.

There's risk—not life-threatening risk, but risk to our person just the same. It's exciting and challenging.

Sports bring us together with our teammates in ways nothing else can. They also force us to deal with our opponents. We may consider them enemies in one sense, but ultimately we have to deal with them as fellow athletes. We have to have a philosophy of sportsmanship. And that's something that's a little different with all of us.

Someone said that only in war and prison do we find out the true character of a man. But I think sports do the same thing for us—in a much healthier environment than war or prison. Sports not only reveal character, they can be used as a tool to build it.

Winning is great. The thrill of victory. The sense of accomplishment. The affirmation of the crowd. But it's the losses that take us to the edge.

I hate to lose—with a passion. There are times after a loss when I hate the very game itself. There are few things in life that can match my revulsion at losing. I would have given up sports a long time ago had I not learned how to rebound from defeat and frustration, had I not developed a highly refined system of trained recovery . . . had I not discovered the strategies of turning defeat into victory.

Typical Jock: It ain't nothin' but something to do.
Train Tough Attitude: It's turning defeat into victory.

Five Great Philosophic Sports Issues
You Can't Win Them All

Why not?

Didn't the '72 Miami Dolphins go 17–0?

Sure, a 162-game baseball schedule or 82-game basketball schedule makes it tough. But which of those games are you willing to concede? You've got to try like crazy to win them all.

"You can't win them all" is a cop-out. I prefer, "Sometimes you eat the bear, and sometimes the bear eats you"—that's more what losing feels like.

"You can't win them all" is a throwaway line, one that comes in handy when there's not much else to be said after a loss. It's like taking a couple of aspirin at the onset of a headache. Sometimes it helps, but you've still got to tackle the tough questions if you want to understand the reasons for a loss.

Only then can you set out to "win them all" all over again.

Show Me a Good Loser, and I'll Show You a Loser

This is a derivative quote attributed to the great Knute Rockne, who actually said something even more graceless. It's a fairly useless comment.

Show me a good loser, and I'll show you a guy playing golf with his boss.

Is a poor loser any less a loser?

I don't like the term *loser* to begin with. A loser is someone who goes out of his way to find a way to lose, who's compulsive about it. There aren't many of those on a sports field. Most of us are trying hard to win, and mixed results do not a loser make.

Success is matter of averages, not absolutes. Mickey Mantle hit 536 home runs; he also struck out 1,710 times. Sports are rarely an all-or-nothing proposition.

A loss always has hidden assets. We can learn from defeat. Defeat shows us our weaknesses and mistakes in a way that victory masks. And when we see them, we can fix them. If at first you don't succeed, find out why.

Own up to your shortcomings. Lessen negative emotions. Get over it, so you can get on with it. Accepting loss is part of character; accepting second-best effort is not.

Develop a system of recovery from a loss. Congratulate the winner. Spend some time alone. Talk it out with a coach or teammate. Devise your plan for a comeback.

Keep doing the things that winners do, and you'll spend a lot less time being a good loser.

Giving 110 Percent

I used to maintain that 100 percent was all a player could give. Then I did the math.

You get 100 percent for all-out effort.

You get the other 10 percent for finding additional areas in which to make effort. You're working harder and smarter. That's giving 110 percent.

Winning Isn't Everything, It's the Only Thing

This isn't my favorite quote—often attributed to Vince Lombardi. One of the greatest motivational coaches ever, Coach Lombardi probably wishes he didn't get the credit for this one. Most of his stuff is right on. Try this one for size:

> Winning is not a sometime thing; it's an all-the-time thing. You don't win once in a while; you don't do things right once in a while; you do them right all the time. Winning is a habit.

Now that one really works for me. But the "winning is the only thing" business is too easily misinterpreted. Winning isn't always what shows up on the scoreboard, and we're usually not as good as we think we are when we win—or as bad as we feel when we lose.

On a practical level, winning *is* the only thing. That's how you have to think. When you're focused on the mission—winning—you take care of everything else in its proper context. Every little thing either contributes to winning or becomes a stumbling block to winning.

When a part of your life is out of balance, you have to readjust to get back on the winning track.

In a sense, sports are about the journey as well as the destination. If you win all the time but everything else is broken—what good is that? There does need to be a balance. The journey and the destination can merge.

Going all out for the win keeps you pointed in the right direction. If your destination is Chicago, you don't want to wind up in Detroit. It's OK to enjoy the journey, just make sure you're pointed toward the win.

It's Not Whether You Win or Lose, but How You Play the Game

This old saying is another misquote from one of the greatest sports writers of all time—Grantland Rice. Here's what he really said:

> For when the One Great Scorer comes to write against your name—
> He marks—not that you won or lost—but how you played the game.

The truth is that no matter how focused we are on winning and how hard we work toward it, we can't *command* a winning outcome. Best effort and a clean conscience are things you can control.

If you lost a bowl game because you partied the night before, there are regrets. There are few regrets when you do your best. You can assess your performance without fear or recrimination. Your effort alone has an intrinsic value, and you can step away from seeing it only in relation to others. I can't be Kobe Bryant. But I can be a very tough Mark Bender.

I call it my "no-regrets" philosophy. I prepare. I play all out, all the time. I play to win, but I can live with my best effort—which includes continually learning from mistakes and looking for new ways to win.

"No regrets" carries over to every single action on the field of play. There is no frustration after failed attempts; there is only refocus on the moment and the immediate future. It's an attitude the One Great Scorer can appreciate.

I think we're getting pretty close to the meaning of life here.

The Softball Prayer

Last year I played my first season of church league softball. Pine Ridge Presbyterian, for whom I played, was a scrappy outfit. We took to calling ourselves "the Ridge."

The league was very competitive—and enlightening. In most ways it was just like any other league I've played in—the guys played hard with no quarter given. There was probably less swearing, but otherwise things were about the same.

The major difference was the postgame prayer. At the end of every game, both teams shook hands and gathered around the pitcher's mound while a player from the losing team said a prayer. It seemed a bit awkward at first, but then I came to see it as a good way to start the healing process for the loser and add a bit of perspective for the winners.

It wasn't long before the prayers became a bit of a competition in themselves. I hated to lose to First Baptist, but the postgame prayer made it almost worth the pain. Here's what one of my teammates offered up:

Dear Lord, it takes a mountain of a team to take on the Ridge. You know we gave it everything we had. We thank you for these Baptists and what they showed us about teamwork today—doing so much with so little. Continue to give them the victory, Lord, until we meet again.

It was such a beautiful thing. Almost makes me want to cry.

★ 49 HAVE A PHILOSOPHY

Focus on achieving best effort and a clear conscience. Consider my "no-regrets" philosophy. Prepare. Play all out, all the time. Play to win, but accept best effort—which includes continually learning from mistakes and looking for new ways to win. "No regrets" carries over to every single action on the field of play. There is no frustration after failed attempts; there is only refocus on the moment and the immediate future. It's fearless.

From the Agony of Defeat to the Thrill of Victory

It's different on the battlefield.

Sports prepare us for combat, and indeed simulate some of the conditions of combat. In sports we learn confidence, teamwork, and perseverance. We perform under conditions of stress, fatigue, and uncertainty. We play to win.

But still, it's different on the battlefield. The depth of the stress, fatigue, and uncertainty is beyond anything you'll find on a sports field. And there's also the horror.

I hope that nothing in this book will be misconstrued as glamorizing war. By the same token, I feel that as athletes we can learn and draw inspiration from our fellow warriors. They perform where the consequences are life and death, where the margin for error is very small, where mistakes are paid for in blood. With the fate of nations at stake, armies play for keeps. And democratic nations are the masters of the come-from-behind victory.

Slim understood the military adage that stands up well in sports and warfare: know your enemy.

Take the World War II battle for Burma, for instance. It's one of my favorites.

The battle began in December 1941, the same month as the Japanese attack on Pearl Harbor. Only this time it was the British who were caught unawares. There was little expectation that the Japanese would attack and little thought given to who would be responsible for meeting it. Intelligence was poor. When the battle was joined, the Japanese thrust did not come where it was expected. The result was disaster.

British forces beat a hasty retreat, trying desperately to break through to the Sittang railway bridge where they might safely cross the six-hundred-yard-wide Sittang River. But the powerful Japanese attacked into their flank, cutting the British force in two. One-third held the bridge, while the remaining two-thirds fought desperately to link up and attempt a crossing.

Then came tragedy. The British commander was awakened at night and told that the bridge could no longer be held. His choice was a difficult one: risk having the bridge fall into Japanese hands, creating an open path for the enemy to take the Burmese capital of Rangoon, or blow it up and cut off his forces on the other side.

He gave the order to blow up the bridge.

The cut-off British soldiers destroyed what they could of their guns and vehicles, stripped, and began the six-hundred-yard swim. Many drowned; others were shot and killed. Fewer than two thousand made it to the other side, mostly in their underwear. Thus ended the decisive battle of what came to be known as "the First Campaign."

Enter Viscount William Slim.

Slim, given command of British forces in Burma, found gunners who had lost their guns, staffs formed from broken units, and odd groups and individuals. "The British looked worried, the Indians puzzled, and the Burmese sulky," he wrote.

There was much to be worried, puzzled, and sulky about. In addition to the general uncertainty of the situation, the British were below strength in men and equipment and poorly trained for jungle combat. The Japanese traveled light and moved with relative ease through supposedly impenetrable jungle. Nearly all British movement was by road or rail, making them subject to the Japanese technique of roadblock and ambush—for which the British had no answer. Morale was the most serious problem of all. Retreats, shortages, and "stories of Japanese supermen" had taken their toll. "There were a lot of badly shaken people about," Slim noted.

Slim demanded discipline.

But it was not the first time William Slim had been asked to turn a situation around. He relished grappling with "problem after problem" and the "tingling of the nerves and the lightening of the spirit, as the urge to get out and tackle the job takes hold."

Slim was a student of warfare who believed that thoughtful analysis might save the day. It soon became apparent that just holding ground would not be enough; the British must find a way to wrest the initiative from the Japanese. They must counterattack at the earliest opportunity and deal a blow hard enough to throw their enemy off balance.

Slim understood the military adage that stands up well in sports and warfare: know your enemy. He learned that the Japanese usually moved with only nine days of supplies and that if they could be held off for that nine days they were extremely vulnerable. Further, the Japanese were bold and effective when their plans went well, but they were slow to readjust and confused when things went wrong. Their leaders would not admit mistakes and would continue to issue follow-up orders that the situation made absurd. Slim thought he could make them pay for this lack of flexibility.

He gave his subordinate commanders the freedom to act on their own—in accordance with his overall intention. He wanted them to be able to react swiftly to changing situations without waiting for a decision from him.

Slim demanded discipline. He found it essential in jungle warfare, where men fought in small groups and the temptation to just hide out was ever-present. He believed in "smartness of turn-out"—what he called "alertness of carriage, cleanliness of person, saluting, and precision of movement." He reinstilled pride in his army.

The British strained to bring every possible asset into the fight. Day after day, often in hand-to-hand combat, they wore the enemy down in a battle of attrition. Gradually, with increasing intensity, they went over to the attack. When the Japanese broke, the British relentlessly pursued. By the end of the conflict, Slim's men were routing the Japanese, killing the enemy at the rate of one hundred to one.

William Slim was promoted to the rank of field marshal. He and his men perfected strategies that redefined modern warfare.

Slim wrote a book about it. He called it *Defeat into Victory*.

Trophies and Scars

The house I live in has to have two things: a driveway suitable for a basketball goal and a room dedicated to Ping-Pong. Both will get plenty of use. It's in the Ping-Pong room where my trophies gather dust. And for every one gathering dust, there are another three packed somewhere in boxes. Most of them don't mean much at this point. It's hard to recall which ones are from which seasons and with which

---

50 TURN DEFEATS INTO VICTORIES

Train yourself to rebound from defeat and frustration with a personal system of trained recovery. Success is a matter of averages, not absolutes. Sports are rarely an all-or-nothing proposition. A loss always has hidden assets. Defeat shows us our weaknesses and mistakes in a way that victory masks. And when we see them, we can fix them. If at first you don't succeed, find out why. Own up to your shortcomings. Set aside negative emotions. Get over it, so you can get on with it. Accepting loss is part of character; accepting second-best effort is not.

---

teammates. I know guys that display them for a year and then throw them away.

It's the scars on my body that have meaning. You never forget a scar. It's something you carry with you, each one a testament to courage or stupidity and the chance encounters with pain and injury that come with a lifetime of seasons and competitions.

The trophies I can't take with me, but the scars I'll wear to my grave.

You can't be a warrior without some scars. You can't enjoy the fruits of victory without having tasted defeat. The arena rewards those who suffer its trials and yet go forth . . . and do great things.

TRAIN TOUGH CHALLENGE

- Practice turning defeats of all kinds into victories.

- Develop a system of recovering from a loss.

- Work harder and smarter—that's 110 percent.

- Adopt the "no-regrets" philosophy. Prepare. Play all out, all the time.

GO FORTH AND
DO GREAT THINGS

In forty hours I shall be in battle, with little information, and on the spur of the moment will have to make the most momentous decisions, but I believe that one's spirit enlarges with responsibility and that, with God's help, I shall make them and make them right.

—GENERAL GEORGE S. PATTON

With God's help. Even the earthy George S. Patton acknowledged the Almighty. "There are no atheists in foxholes," someone once said. Yes, there are situations that are beyond our capabilities in difficulty or magnitude, where we have to call on something larger than ourselves for help. The sooner that process starts, the better.

Find something big to play for. It's important to be inspired. Watch the movie *Hoosiers* before your basketball season, or watch the Navy SEALs training series before the start of football. Play for the little kid in the stands who will see you play only this one time or for the handicapped kid who looks up to you. Find inspiration in everything.

The Train Tough philosophy teaches that strategy and tactics are key. So here's a list of the 50-plus strategies to review. These strategies aren't just theory; they've worked for me and for countless successful athletes I've studied. Using some of them will make you a better athlete, but if you use all of them, you'll find, like General Patton, that your spirit is enlarged and you're ready to take on the world!

The 50 Train Tough Strategies

1. Train Tough. The Train Tough strategy is a powerful way of thinking—based on the way soldiers going into combat need to think. The strategy controls everything. The strategy will take you from "see what happens" to "make it happen." It uses every factor affecting outcome and turns it to your advantage. It's always looking for that edge . . . regardless of what sport you play.

2. Select a Target. As an athlete, target selection is part of your job. It's your job to define your destination and develop a strategy for getting there. Your destination is where you want to be, not a mythical maybe-land of see-what-happens. Once you know the target, you can focus your efforts on hitting it—and blasting through to the other side.

3. Take the High Road. There's a moral aspect to the Train Tough strategy. Your morals. When the conscience buzzer goes off, you have to make the call. The boundaries are there; you have to negotiate the gray areas. The strategy can't provide character, but it does recognize the need for it. We all have to live with ourselves and the society we create by our actions. We play hard. We have the attitude of the warrior. But we keep it on the high road.

4. Make It a Habit. Good habits strengthen performance; bad habits add friction that makes achievement difficult. Every habit builds on every other habit. Good training habits make for good study and career habits. Good sportsmanship habits make for good citizenship habits. Identify, break down, and destroy bad habits; identify, build, and reinforce good habits.

5. Give 110 Percent. This level of effort cannot be proven; it exists only as a very powerful idea. It lifts human effort beyond the quantifiable to a whole new level. Imagination is there. Creativity is there. Finding a better way is there. Go there sometime. Soon.

6. Be a Warrior. Becoming a dedicated athlete is not an easy decision—but it's a choice that leads to extraordinary results. Dedicated athletes are like warriors. Warriors proceed as though the limits of their abilities do not exist. Most athletes try. Warriors don't just try. They perform as though their lives depend on success.

7. Want It Bad. If you want something badly enough, you find a way to get it. You close off distractions and concentrate on the task. Your mind is right. Your desire is focused.

8. Get in the Stance. In action sports, you want to have that middle linebacker attitude. Get in the stance, Baby. Put your body on the altar of sacrifice and look for something to hit. You're the hitter, not the hittee! Posture and bearing affect thought patterns. Confidence exudes confidence.

9. Harness Fear. There are times when we're all scared silly. It can be scary out there, regardless of what sport you're playing. But the issue is not whether we feel fear but how we act in spite of the fear. Used correctly, fear becomes a motivator, a powerful emotion you can harness for peak performance. Don't even try to hide from fear—respond to it!

10. Get Your Act Together. And sometimes that's what it is— an act. You're acting tough and in control in order to function that way. In most sports you're actually performing only a small percentage of the time. The rest of the time you're either standing around wondering, or you're asserting yourself and getting ready. Get ready. After you've played tough for a couple of outings, you'll realize something very important—you're tougher than woodpecker lips.

11. Do the Work. The most direct route to the deserve-it mentality is to do the work. Teams that are honestly convinced that they have worked harder and smarter than the competition can also be convinced that they deserve to win. They're more invested. When they see that their investment is larger, they realize that the stakes are greater for them. They have more to lose; they gain more by winning.

12. Set High Goals. Teams and individual players need goals. Then they need to ask the question, "What will it take to achieve the goals?" The answer always involves a tremendous amount of work.

If it doesn't, then the goals aren't high enough. Lofty goals have high requirements.

13. Commit to Learning. Learning is a commitment. Knowledge and new skills do not just rub off on you because you happen to be in a classroom or gym. You have to rub them in, and that takes energy and dedication. For most of us, it's painful. Too bad, you've got to take the pain. After a while, if you stick with it, it gets easier. It becomes a habit. Take responsibility for your own learning. Don't lay it on the coach. Don't expect it to just happen. You've got to make it happen. Rise above the excuses that it's boring or it won't work. Make it work.

14. Be Coachable. When somebody points out a problem or a weakness you have, accept it. Be open. Be coachable. Don't take it personally. Getting defensive is taking a step away from the reality you need to confront. The truth eventually comes out in the sporting world—usually during the game. Get it out before then, so you can learn from it.

15. Prepare Over Time. You can't cram for tryouts like you can for a world history exam. There are no multiple-choice questions. You've got to prepare over time. Tryouts are where the planned approach pays off. Show up in top shape, having honed your fundamentals. Then you've got a chance.

16. Be Versatile. Demonstrate versatility. Be a guy who can play anywhere; it gives the coach more options for keeping you.

17. Practice Hard. You have to have a work ethic, a set of habits on which to establish your practice strategy. If you pace yourself in practice, you aren't hustling. Unconsciously, you'll do the same thing in a game. You get what you practice. So practice hustling.

18. Don't Repeat Mistakes. Learn the correct fundamentals, and practice performing them correctly. When you learn mistakes, you actually have to backtrack in order to unlearn them. Life is too short for that kind of process.

19. Communicate. The most important way of communicating with your teammates is to honor the team standards by exceeding them. That means showing up early and staying late. That means running your wind sprints past the finish line. In everything you do, you project a professional image and work ethic. Communication with your teammates should be positive and complimentary. Go out of your way to say hi, and smile when you say it. These are the people who are going to make your day. You ought to be happy to see them. Then do your job. That's what your teammates expect.

20. Get on Board. Collective will is like a freight train roaring down the track at a hundred miles an hour. Better get out of the way. When a team has players with willpower, that willpower can become collective will. It's unstoppable.

21. Lead the Way. Think of yourself as a leader. Demonstrate leadership by the way you conduct yourself. Quiet at first, and deferential, you slowly but powerfully exert the force of your personality on others. You accomplish this by doing—by demonstrating that you have control of yourself and are fit to lead others. Leadership is a trust that is earned.

22. Be a Competitor. Leaders challenge teammates to compete. They communicate the message verbally and nonverbally, by what they say and what they do. Competitiveness takes audacity. Competitiveness is audacity applied to the quest of winning, the animal desire to get it on with a worthy opponent, to match the attack blow for blow. It's using your opponent to drive you to ever-increasing heights of performance. It is not for the faint of heart. Leaders have competitiveness in spades.

23. Pick Yourself Up. Leaders fall, and leaders fail. They strike out, fumble, and drop the ball. There's always a bit of extra trauma when leaders fail. But when you're a leader, you can't let it get to you. You can't quit, not even for a minute. Players will accept the leader's failing; after all, they accept that leaders are human. But they will not respect leaders who quit. The leader must keep his game face. He must demonstrate resiliency, both mentally and physically. Mentally, he must immediately show that his spirit has not been broken. Physically, he must demonstrate his continued commitment to perform. Leaders play through the tough moments, gathering energy from the challenge. Their teammates will follow.

24. Know Your Enemy. The idea is to know your enemy's tactics, weaponry, and thinking so that you can take advantage of him. You want to get inside his head and learn how he reacts, makes decisions, and operates. That way you can protect yourself, deceive him about your true intentions, and create surprise by doing something he doesn't expect. Remember, the whole point of knowing your enemy is so you can run your game on him. Never lose focus on what you have to do. You want to make your enemy play your game.

25. Never, *Ever* Underestimate an Opponent. There's no such thing as an easy one. All opponents are dangerous. There are many ways to die on the battlefield and many ways to be surprised on the field of play. Respect your opponent. Respect the fact that he's trying to defeat you. That makes him dangerous. By the same token, don't make him 10 feet tall.

26. Build a Case for Yourself. Accept responsibility for determining your own mind-set. It's part of your job. It's called mental toughness. Build a case for yourself. Your level of achievement is tied to the self-concept that you build—performance is a self-fulfilling prophecy. Approach every game in the same workmanlike manner, building solid work habits that will hold you up when the going gets tough.

27. Visualize It. Focus both positive thinking and willpower to achieve maximum benefit. Visualization is your means to bringing these two together. In focus time number one you define the mission. In focus time number two you reinforce the specific objectives. By uniting positive thinking and willpower in your imagination, you produce a new and dynamic performance power.

28. Experience the Future. Through the vehicle of visualization, you can journey to the future—see it, feel it, and affect it. Instead of worrying about it or wasting psychic energy getting unduly hyped for it, you can let it come to you. You're ready for takeoff, certain of your ability and free from doubt.

29. Laser Focus. Know what to expect. Be ready for those nanoseconds of opportunity. Let your desire drive focus. Focus knows no fear. It's nonjudgmental. Focus takes you to the zone, that place every athlete dreams about. When you're taking care of business you can accept yourself and your performance for what they are. You're doing your best, and you're at your best. It doesn't get any better.

30. Understand Momentum. Most games have waves of momentum, with the advantage shifting from team to team. Your objective is to ride your team's positive waves all the way to the beach. And conversely, you must find ways to upset your opponents' rhythm when things are going their way. Start the game strong. When ahead, keep the pressure on. When the going gets tough, attack! Staging a comeback is like starting a fire. It begins with a spark, flickers a bit, ignites, begins burning, requires stoking, and then builds so much heat that it consumes everything in its path.

31. Plan on Crunch Time. It's going to happen. You need to be ready. Consciously identify crunch-time moments, and commit to coming through. That way you're primed for success instead of being surprised by opportunity. Crunch time is what we dream about. Be ready for it.

32. Stay in the Moment. It's not enough to be there, you have to be all the way there. You've front-end loaded all the magnitude stuff. You're radiating confidence. You know it's crunch time, and you've committed to coming through. So *be* where you are in the process. *Stay in the moment.*

33. Understand the System. Sports mirror life. In fact, sports mirror the ugliest part of life. You hunt; you're hunted. You win; you lose. And a lot of heavy stuff happens in between. It's a jungle. Decide who you want to be out there. Do you want to be a good guy? Or a bad guy? What actions are acceptable to you? Where do you draw the line? Don't kid yourself. Understand the system.

34. Prove Your Merit. Proving merit is about courage—courage in the face of adversity and risk. It's about physical prowess and often the ability to play through pain and the fear of injury. Earning the peak experience is what it's all about. The arena gives us the chance to get there, to experience that feeling of invincibility, when no one can stop you.

35. Dominate. It takes a unique set of circumstances for a team to dominate over a season or a number of years. It takes extraordinary players with a team orientation, superb coaching, dedication, and a sustainable reason for confidence.

36. Beat the Odds. What does it take for an underdog to win? Preparation. Determination. Leadership. Surprise.

37. Have Some Heroes. Go ahead, have some heroes. Identify with them; be a bit of a fan. Get yourself inspired. Realizing they're human, study their magic moments, how they performed as underdogs, how they performed under pressure, and how they built dynasties. Don't fall for the fallacy that heroes have it made. Remember something else: the obstacles they had to overcome.

38. Save the Party. Some athletes put as much emphasis on their social life as they do on their sport. Some of them get away with it. But would they be more effective if they had themselves more under control? The answer is "yes!" Every time. Save the party for after you've won the championship.

39. Just Say "No." When it comes to gambling, drunkenness, illegal drug use, steroids, and tobacco the answer is obvious. Keep it real simple on this one. Just say "no."

40. Embrace Change. Both the culture and the sports world are changing at warp speed. The increasing presence of women in sports will continue to amaze as opportunities expand. Get used to it. The only thing constant will be change. Enjoy the ride.

41. Supercondition. Almost all world-class athletic achievement comes as a result of superconditioning. You can cover a lot of shortcomings with conditioning. Tailor your conditioning program to the sport you play, and learn the correct techniques for what you're doing. Commit to being in superior shape to your competition. It'll pay off when they quit and you're still pushing.

42. Stay in the Band of Excellence. With any conditioning program, it's important to establish a base and keep yourself in the band of excellence. Even when you're in a down period—and all of us have them—don't let yourself get to the point where you have to start over. Find the time to do what needs to be done. Use simple exercises, like push-ups and sit-ups, to keep you grounded.

43. Kick Bad Habits; Replace with Good. Half of establishing a healthy diet is getting rid of bad habits; the other half is establishing good ones. Apply common sense, along with the basics of what you recall from eighth-grade health class. Drink more water; get more rest. Out with the bad habits, in with the good.

44. Hype Out. Use the hyper home workout to give you an idea of what it's like to perform in the hyper zone. Set up a private area with your favorite workout toys: dumbbells, barbells, whatever. Find your most raucous CD, and crank up the volume. Now get to work. Exceed your normal workout by 20 percent.

45. Get Hyped. Agitate. Project energy. Go over the top, above the zone, and into the hyper state. Attack. Attack. Attack!

46. Aim for Your Finest Hour. Can you imagine what it's like to play with a finest-hour attitude? To convey the attitude that you'll never quit and never give in? Imagine what kind of message that sends to the other team? It's almost crazy. It's the attitude that gets you back up when you've been knocked down, that keeps you on the field when the others are showing those subtle signs of quitting. It's being tough-minded and believing you can overcome any obstacle.

47. Return to Simple Action. When things get tough, start doing the little things right. Focus on executing each fundamental with single-point attention. Let go of results. Do each step of the process to the very best of your ability—and stay positive.

48. Expect a Few Smacks in the Eye. "There are no safe battles," said Winston Churchill. Success depends on taking calculated risks in the face of adversity. You're going to get knocked down and smacked around. Expect it. Soldier through it, and counterattack. The reward for painful, relentless effort is victory.

49. Have a Philosophy. Focus on achieving best effort and a clear conscience. Consider my "no-regrets" philosophy. Prepare. Play all out, all the time. Play to win, but accept best effort—which includes continually learning from mistakes and looking for new ways to win. "No regrets" carries over to every single action on the field of play. There is no frustration after failed attempts; there is only refocus on the moment and the immediate future. It's fearless.

50. Turn Defeats into Victories. Train yourself to rebound from defeat and frustration with a personal system of trained recovery. Success is a matter of averages, not absolutes. Sports are rarely an all-or-nothing proposition. A loss always has hidden assets. Defeat shows us our weaknesses and mistakes in a way that victory masks. And when we see them, we can fix them. If at first you don't succeed, find out why. Own up to your shortcomings. Set aside negative emotions. Get over it, so you can get on with it. Accepting loss is part of character; accepting second-best effort is not.

51. Be Inspired. Find something big to play for. It's important to be inspired. Watch the movie *Hoosiers* before your basketball season, or watch the Navy SEALs training series before the start of football. Play for the little kid in the stands who will see you play only this one time or for the handicapped kid who looks up to you. Find inspiration in everything.

OK, so there are 51. Which one would you leave out? I couldn't decide either. They're all important, even though you might challenge some of them.

Challenge whatever you want! Ultimately, you have to do your own thinking and find out for yourself what works for you. The things you discover on your own will be infinitely more valuable than anything anyone else can tell you. Some things you have to experience for yourself.

But you've gotten your money's worth. You've megadosed all the right psychic vitamins.

It's almost time to go out and do great things. Just give me a few more lines to get you on your way.

Be tough on yourself.

Sure, the way is hard, but if you live in the free world, it's been made a lot easier by the men and women who have gone on before, many of whom wore the uniform of their team—and their country.

Take Ted Williams, for instance—the last man to hit .400 in the major leagues. Ted hit .406 in 1941, dropped to .356 in 1942, then dropped out of sight serving his country in 1943, 1944, and 1945 during World War II. He was called up again for the Korean War after six games of the 1952 season. He was hitting .400 at the time.

Unlike many ballplayers who played on service teams during the war, Williams was a pilot who flew combat missions over Korea. On one combat mission he was hit by small arms fire, crash-landed his crippled jet, and escaped from the flaming wreckage.

Returning to the big leagues in 1953 at age 35, Williams was thought to be washed up. He homered in his first at-bat in Fenway Park and never looked back, hitting .407 for the 37 games he played that season. He would play seven more years, finishing his career with 521 home runs and a .344 batting average—and he gave nearly five years of his prime defending America.

Then consider the contributions of black athletes who made the same sacrifices while being denied their full rights as citizens.

Take Spotswood Poles for example. A switch-hitting outfielder, Poles was the fastest player of his era, and perhaps the fastest of all time. He hit .487 for the New York Lincoln Giants of the Negro Leagues in 1914. In 10 exhibition games against white major league teams he hit .610.

Spotswood Poles joined the Negro Regiment of Infantry in World War I, the famous 369th Infantry Regiment. "Harlem's Own" was the only volunteer regiment raised for war to actually reach France.

When American units refused to serve alongside them, the 369th was "assigned" to the French Fourth Army. There they spent 191 days in combat, the longest of any American regiment in the war. The 369th was cited for bravery 11 times, and the entire regiment received the French Croix de Guerre for gallantry under fire. They never had a man captured and never lost a foot of ground. The Germans called them "hellfighters." Their musicians introduced jazz to Europe.

Spotswood Poles earned five battle stars and the Purple Heart. He is buried in Arlington National Cemetery.

Thousands of black Americans again served their country in segregated units in World War II. Ralph Johnson, a pitcher for the Philadelphia Stars, never made it back. But a bunch of his fellow Negro Leaguers beat George Patton's Third Army baseball team after the war in Hitler's Nuremburg Stadium. And Patton didn't like to lose.

It wasn't until 1947 that Jackie Robinson broke through the color line in major league baseball. A year later Harry Truman ended segregation of the armed forces by executive order.

And you thought you had it rough.

From the Roman arena to the Negro Leagues, our forebears have left us a legacy of courage.

It's hard for those of us who play sports today to realize the depth of dedication and sacrifice of the athletes who came before. It's up to us to add our contribution, in some small way, to that legacy. It's up to us to go out and do great things, whether on the playing field or on the battlefield, if called. The successful attitudes, tactics, and strategies are similar. I pray that your heroics will be called for only on the playing field. The Train Tough skills you master there will be of benefit anywhere in life.

As for me, I plan to play on for a few more years. I hope to see you out there.

Maybe you'll yell to me what General Patton yelled to General Rommel as he kicked the German army across North Africa:

"I read your book!"

Now get out there.

51 BE INSPIRED

Find something big to play for. It's important to be inspired. Watch the movie *Hoosiers* before your basketball season, or watch the Navy SEALs training series before the start of football. Play for the little kid in the stands who will see you play only this one time or for the handicapped kid who looks up to you. Find inspiration in everything.

ABOUT THE AUTHOR

LIEUTENANT COLONEL (RET.) MARK BENDER is the author and guiding light of the Train Tough strategies. A much-in-demand motivational speaker, Bender has spoken to numerous sports teams, including the New York Yankees baseball team. He has been interviewed on radio from coast to coast, and his comedy has entertained live audiences in the United States and Europe.

A 1996 graduate of the U.S. Army War College, Bender holds a graduate degree in military art and science and is the author of *Watershed at Leavenworth* (CSI), the dynamic story of Dwight Eisenhower's rise to power after graduating first in his class at the Army's Command and General Staff College. *Watershed* details the strategies and tactics Eisenhower employed in mastering the highly competitive yearlong course, a course his superiors told him he would "probably fail." Bender borrows heavily from his own military experience in analyzing the Eisenhower strategy and has appeared as a subject matter expert on A&E's *Biography*.

His recent book, *Trial by Basketball: The Life and Times of Tex Winter* (ADDAX), took him inside the Chicago Bulls dynasty years while he explored the life of the master architect of the famed triangle offense. *Trial* provided an in-depth analysis of the Michael Jordan phenomenon, the bittersweet presence of Dennis Rodman, and the migration of a coaching staff to Tinseltown—and a world championship. Los Angeles Lakers coach Phil Jackson wrote the foreword to *Trial*, and Mark was one of the few persons allowed into his Lakers basketball practices.

Bender recently completed his 75th season in team sports. He has served internationally as a sports officer and was named a NATO Officer of the Year for his innovative sports programs. Baseball, basketball, and volleyball are his mainstays—but he also brings experience from football, soccer, wrestling, European handball, sprints and distance running, weight lifting, golf, and tennis. If it's a sport, Bender has played it, coached it, and figured out how to win at it. He integrated volleyball into the Army's premier junior executive college and was named the school's Instructor of the Year in 1994. A physical fitness fanatic, he achieved the Army's maximum physical fitness score for 17 consecutive years.

Still an active competitor in his fifties, Bender has a breadth of sporting experience few can match. He communicates his Train Tough strategies with a unique style . . . and the confidence of someone who's been there. For further information on the author, visit www.traintough.com.